Living With Messages from Heaven

A Guide to Conversations with the Beyond

Rebecca Anne LoCicero

BALBOA.
PRESS

A DIVISION OF HAY HOUSE

Website - www.RebeccaAnne.org

Balboa Press books may be ordered through booksellers or by contacting:

Balboa Press
A Division of Hay House
1663 Liberty Drive
Bloomington, IN 47403
www.balboapress.com
1 (877) 407-4847

Because of the dynamic nature of the Internet, any web addresses or links contained in
this book may have changed since publication and may no longer be valid. The views
expressed in this work are solely those of the author and do not necessarily reflect the
views of the publisher, and the publisher hereby disclaims any responsibility for them.

The author of this book does not dispense medical advice or prescribe the use of any
technique as a form of treatment for physical, emotional, or medical problems without the
advice of a physician, either directly or indirectly. The intent of the author is only to offer
information of a general nature to help you in your quest for emotional and spiritual well-
being. In the event you use any of the information in this book for yourself, which is your
constitutional right, the author and the publisher assume no responsibility for your actions.

Any people depicted in stock imagery provided by Thinkstock are models,
and such images are being used for illustrative purposes only.
Certain stock imagery © Thinkstock.

Printed in the United States of America.

ISBN: 978-1-4525-2283-8 (sc)
ISBN: 978-1-4525-2284-5 (e)

Library of Congress Control Number: 2014917272

Balboa Press rev. date: 09/25/2014

This book was written by Rebecca Anne LoCicero as an Advocate for Psychic Mediumship and Prophets in the Millennium

For Julia*Ronald*Nora

And with special dedication to all my
friends & family "there" in Heaven!

Contents

Chapter 1

An Introduction

I am in a constant state of learning and discerning. In no way is this book my end-all opinion, however, it does reflect, quite clearly, my current standing on issues related to the term "psychic medium". I am a psychic medium; at least this is what I call one aspect of myself. There are a lot of words to describe what it is that I do. For example: prophet, seer, gypsy, fortune-teller, clairvoyant, reader, oracle, channeler, intuitive, etc. I have heard some call me an evildoer, bad witch and other not-so-pleasant names. I do understand that, where there is a fear of the unknown or strict religious foundations, the unpleasant terms could arise. With a clear explanation and understanding of what I do, I hope to educate those who do not understand what the millennium perception of the words 'psychic medium' means. I hope to convey what a sense of joy and peace surrounds the whole term.

Know up front that I do not teach just one technique; I teach no new modalities. The gifts and abilities that a psychic medium has would not fit into one small box or one simple definition. This book is not a class, or a lesson; it is an awakening of the awareness that there is a connection to the

1

beyond. This book is not an instruction manual as much as it is a resource of truths and beliefs, guidelines and information. Even though I have taken many classes from a variety of resources and even consider myself an expert in some areas, I commit myself to the belief that there is not one specific way to connect to your intuition. The ways are limitless. I am a psychic medium so I am guiding and mentoring others along their paths to enlightenment with every client I connect for. That is a big responsibility and one that I have learned to grasp onto as I have become more experienced in this field of work. I know there are many of us who are on that same mission in life while guiding others in the way of their soul. This book will share with you more in-depth information in that area. I believe that all modalities are already within our gifts and abilities as they resonate with our souls. We were born with the gift to connect to Heaven, to information, to our loved ones who have crossed. That ability lies within and always has. It is more a time to awaken to that realization then to analyze the idea of it. I present myself as a guide to others to open up and then to guide themselves within their own gifts. This is an area where Spirit dwells, God is present and there is no judgment.

There are many aspects to the term psychic medium. I believe, first and foremost, that being a psychic medium is a gift for our human experience; it is a spiritual connection. It is not, however, my only reason or explanation for my gifts. Religious experiences and mystical forces have great influences on my opinions however, it does not end there. It is a strong connection to energy, free will and science, all connected to consciousness, experience and open-mindedness.

It is knowledge and education, memories and physiological experiences all connected together.

The title "psychic medium" goes beyond just the words. It is a gift, but it is also an ability which is treated like any other ability. If you like the piano and have a gift to play piano, you should take lessons, practice, and continue to play and practice to keep your ability fresh. Some may be born with the talent as well. Is that a gift? Is that an ability? I believe it is both and with that gift comes focused direction to produce and prosper within that ability. Having the ability to "know" as a psychic medium does should be treated like ability and nurtured through classes, prayer, meditation and research to understand the purpose of the ability. There is always purpose behind the information that is received. It is also considered ability due to the fact that it is a physical and scientific energetic process. It does affect body and mind in ways that are beyond just the "spiritual" connection. It is a process involving our total being. As a psychic medium, when receiving information, there are times when the human body takes a toll. I often describe it as running. You can go so far for so long and when the time comes for you to stop, there is that adrenalin rush, the "runner's high," and your body is tired and drained. There is a need to relax, unwind, reclaim your energy and rejuvenate one's own personal power to be able to continue in this line of work.

Taking the title of a "psychic medium" into one's life to share with others is a huge life choice. When sharing with your family, friends, or local circles that you have abilities brings about opinions from everyone. If you choose to state that you are a psychic medium, you have to be totally comfortable and knowledgeable about what you are claiming. It is a process of acceptance; it is not just about others accepting you. First, it must be all about you. It was about me, what I thought, what I believed, and what I felt was crazy. My Roman Catholic upbringing meant that I had a lot of inner influences that I had to debate with myself before I could fully accept this path as I have. Everyone has a life and they make choices all the time, all day long, and some of these choices have life-long ramifications such as marriage, divorce, health, children and work. Choosing to make your path in life one that holds not just the title of "psychic medium", but also the depth of what it means spiritually is a huge responsibility and should be treated as an important life choice. I believe we are all, on some level, "psychic mediums" as soul-connected human beings. Know that the purpose of this book is not to bring you to choose that you must call yourself a psychic medium and start working and doing readings. It is beyond that! I do believe everyone can connect to their intuition however I do not feel that everyone can or even should do this for work. If you can embrace and encompass this idea of what a psychic medium is and can bring it into your life, you can and will be connected to the beyond energy to advance your soul and purpose here on earth in a profound way. You can come to believe in the signs and connections your loved ones in Heaven are sending you daily!

That life choice does not come without a profound responsibility to others and that, at times, can seem like a burden. One of the reasons why I wanted to write this book is because I am a psychic medium as my full-time business. This is my gift, my ability, my life choice; it is my burden and my responsibility. Basically, it is my Job! It is not a burden as much as it is a love, but it is a burden when you consider that there was really nothing else in life I could do. I tried to be a waitress, receptionist, even a therapist. I had to think about ethics, procedures, choices and advertising. I have to show responsibility with sharing this gift with others. I chose to volunteer, as a spiritual person should, but then also had to consider prices for my readings. I had to make sure that my clients understood what their responsibility was as the one receiving the readings.

So, this is why I wrote this book; to help open an awareness of what options are out there. To share my story and to help others who feel they are where I am now, or was at some point in time. I hope it entertains you. I hope to enlighten and inspire while helping to attune and open others to their intuitive connections. I wrote this book to help those who are questioning the concept of psychic mediums by helping them to understand that it is a beautiful, pure, loving, scientific and especially spiritual term.

"Now is the Time"

Our message, intuition and love for all humanity is a
love in your hearts that is yours to use, when the time
came and you were born, when you were turned to
understanding and enlightenment…Now is the time
Our messages and our love will spread itself out
like an additional positive chain reaction affecting
each human being living and breathing.
We are all looking for that positive
reinforcement…Now is the time
Prepare your children to accept this intuitive world they
are being introduced to. They already have the gift that
they are just now learning about. Nurture that and bring
that to harmony in their environment…Now is the time
Praise the gift of creation for allowing
us to experience such love.
(Rebecca Anne, Channeled Angel Poetry)

Chapter 2

There Are Three Rules to Know Before I Read You; They Are Not "Rules" So Much as They Are Simple Guidelines to Receive the Best Reading You Can

There are three "rules" which I must tell you before I begin any reading sessions. These are guidelines for you to better accept the information in the best way. When I am going to read for a group or an individual the rules are the same.

1. Yes and No. You're here to see what the psychic medium is going to tell you; for the insight and information; for verifiable connections and confirmation. That way, you get to feel as if there is an awesome energy full of connections to the other side; that your loved ones are around watching over you; they are ok and are with you still. So if I say something you understand or agree with, Say YES. That is my way of getting confirmation that I have said something you understand; that what I have received as the messenger matches for you! That is a wonderful surprise to me also at the time. The Yes for verification is always needed. Sometimes you may need to say NO. I am only human, but the information I receive is not

supposed to be wrong. It is supposed to make sense to you and be placed within your mind as understandable accurate connections and messages. If you do not "get it", then say NO. That way I can turn to the spirit and say "Hey, they didn't get it. Can I have it another way?" or at the least know that you don't get it, and ask for more information from Spirit for clarity. It is a "conversation" with the Beyond. I prefer you only say Yes and No if you can! Do not feed me information. As your soul is connecting to me and my soul is connecting to the dead and your soul is also connecting to the other side, we are all in the same space! You will feel what I feel; just let me be the 'medium' and bring it through for you.

2. Here and There. We are here, in skin, alive on Earth, our loved ones in spirit are there, no skin, not here. When they do come through, or any information comes through, it will connect to that which is "here" and "there". The names they share may be of loved ones here they are watching over and/or those who are with them there. If you can open your mind to think of connections in both the here and there, your reading will be expanded and built on in many ways. You will gain a 'knowing' that your loved ones are watching over you here. You will realize that they know what you are doing here. All of this will bring realization to you that they are 'there' with you here, and make the reading a fuller experience for you.

3. Trauma vs. Illness. When I am bringing through someone who has had a trauma, there is an energy that is felt around the crossing. It is not negative, it is different. When someone has died of an illness, that is also an energy felt. I mention this because when I read for you there is a difference

and the dead love to call out and talk about how they died. It is the one thing they didn't get to talk about before then went. The trauma energy may come through intense or with a harsh energy, but it is important to know that they are fine. It is just the way the trauma energy flow is expressed. Also know that your loved ones in spirit are Happy, Healthy and Full of Love at ALL TIMES!

CHAPTER 3

Becoming a Psychic Medium: My Story

P arts of this book are based on the personal experiences which I have had leading me to where I am now. As we all have our story, I too feel that I have formed and evolved to where I am now and that life is perfect in this way. This is my story. It is not a complete picture, but it is a combination of events that I hope will help you to connect to me on an intimate level. I am a normal person. I am a one of a kind! I am a human being just like you and I have the same general responsibilities and experiences. I often describe my adventure as a way to explain how I went from "not normal" to "fully aware."

It was not until I was just into my 30's when I finally confirmed through my mother that I had indeed been talking to and seeing dead people since early childhood. She told me stories about me seeing my grandfather and other relatives including our family poodle who were all passed away at the time I was connecting to them. As a child, about age five, I sat in an auditorium at the grade school and told my mother that my grandfather was walking in the back holding a baby boy. A few weeks later my mother's younger sister gave birth to the last grandson. There were other spiritual encounters in my home with the same grandfather. One time I can clearly remember was the appearance of my grandfather, my sister who was stillborn, and our family poodle together at the top of the stairs. I can still remember seeing this man standing tall, smiling, holding our family pet that had recently passed; next to him this spirit of a little girl, smiling and glowing, standing tall next to our grandfather. I have to admit that I was so profoundly convinced that it did happen that I remember telling my brother, who was home taking care of me at the time. I cannot recall his reaction at this time, but I do remember that I went directly to get the dog's collar and put it on the top of the stairs where this apparition had manifested. I do not remember now if there was a specific message, but I did tell my mother about it when she got home. I knew she had believed in me and I had faith that she would accept my vision.

Now I do believe that the awareness of this psychic ability can run in the family. I have seen it over and over with families of my clients and students. I was unable to have any guidance from a family member, as I was adopted as a baby. My parents are the two best people in the world and I am sure that God placed me with my adoptive parents for a purpose. They guided me to get where I am now, where I needed to be. I am humbled, and have become enlightened in a deeper way, about how there is much purpose to where you are introduced as a human in life. There was a distinct path I had to take, that I was able to take, as a result of where I was divinely placed for my upbringing. All involved parties, with their own spiritual path in the grasp of the situation, intertwined. It is a soul-searching adventure; one I enjoy.

So as I grew up, I can honestly say I was a tough kid. I remember having impressions as a teenager, but mostly ignored or put aside my psychic energy. I can not pinpoint when it was that I stopped talking to my dead relatives, but I know that there were no further energy connections through my teens. I know that must have happened for many reasons, such as learning that I had to experience the real life. I often listened to my "gut instinct" but never realized how right I was at times. I did learn through my school years that I was open and aware as an extremely empathetic person.

I do not have the privilege to doubt that there is an afterlife. Nowhere in my memory is there a moment when I though that maybe we go to the earth and recycle that way and that is the end. I have tried to imagine what life would be like without the connection to spirit, heaven and the beyond all together. It is impossible. In some ways I remember wanting to be able to attached to Darwinism, or Agnostic or anything of the kind. Even in college, when studying different courses on theology, sociology and psychology; at no point could I release for a single second that there was a debate about the afterlife. I was born knowing that death is not the end of our life, and that it is really just barely the beginning.

Once 18 years old, I was off to college where it all came back to me. My roommate "coincidentally" (more like synchronicity) was overly interested in a number of psychic activities. Her friends were working on telepathy, remote viewing and astral projection. I dove right in with her until it filled all of my free time. It was amazing how everything I was learning from 18 to 20 was more important to me then the social work associates degree I was working toward. From Ouija boards to séances on Halloween, we did it all. Those were my "research" years. I was reawakening a small part of that psychic energy. I was educating myself on what was really out there; what to learn from, what to turn away from, how to bring light and keep out the dark. I explored the dark corners of the library where a variety of religious books collided with witchcraft and then the paranormal.

I'll never forget the séance I was a part of during those college years. Can you imagine sitting in a circle of 13 in a very foggy New England soccer field next to a cemetery, on Halloween night? The results of that evening's adventure will never leave my mind. My naïve Catholic mind persuaded me to wear a scapula and a rosary to this event, of which I was one of the ringleaders. We held hands and called in spirits. I knew immediately that this was a bad idea. We were strong energies together; a concept we knew nothing about. We were all putting our intentions in the same place and manifesting by pulling in to us spirits that did not want to communicate. I believe I remember us all getting in trouble with the college administration, if for nothing else but causing fear on campus. We were not doing anything illegal at all, but we were doing something that, at the time, was negative. I am sure that the 13 of us who experienced this rush of energy trying to take control, all have a deeper understanding there are some things out there which you just don't do! I personally look back at that now and wonder just how much of my awareness that I was a medium may have had an effect on the situation. There are experiences you must go through to understand concepts in a deeper way.

I searched and found areas where there was more of a connection to "beyond" and great information there. I was interested in tarot cards and crystals. New Age stores would often host events and psychics. They were, in my mind, brighter resources in a lighter way for the soul to connect the spiritual realms. In the light places I felt better and was able to focus more on my psychic ability. Once you start looking and wondering about the New Age, Wiccan or spiritual world, you will eventually find a psychic. I did. That is how I came to use tarot cards. I had my first set given to me at 19. I was at a psychic's home where she was chain smoking and putting the cards down slowly while puffing with each flip. She was drawing cards in a fashion onto the table, explaining with each, how it will be representative of my life. Each card was a "sword" which is a suit within this deck. Once all the cards were down, she simply looked at them all, looked at me and told me that due to the fact that every card she drew was a sword, it was a sign to her that this was now to be my deck. She picked them all up and handed them to me. She never gave me a reading that day. I am not sure if that happened to her because she was to shift from her cards to another deck and she may have asked for a sign. With all swords appearing, that could have been it. I have no reason to debate or understand the why of it; I just know I wanted that deck. I still have the cards, but I only used them for a few years before I learned that I can do the same work without them. I used the cards to help me focus on more details when reading for someone. I know now that even my friends, who were there for me when I was using the cards and beginning my discovery of beyond information, were there for a reason. I would go over to a friend, Mare; her home was my escape at times where I could freely do my cards, no payment, just fun and learning. We all have people who are there for us when we feel we need to be ourselves. I still pull out the cards once in a while, but I believe I will always feel a better connection without anything to interfere with my channel, at least at this point in time. I moved past those cards due to the fact that the cards became a disruption. I was receiving the energy and information through the cards. Eventually, I came to realize that I was able, as a medium, to channel the information much clearer without having an in-between resource to help me interpret. I considered ordering a blank deck, but my soul was expressing to me that I could do it on my own. I still have a love for all kinds of intuitive, tarot and angel decks. I find them to be fun, inspirational and direct.

I took adult education courses and met psychic and intuitive mentors, started a business and charged for readings, psychic parties, entertainment agency gigs and more. I met Mary, my core mentor and teacher, who is someone I feel is a beautiful guide to me here on earth and who naturally brings love and awareness through her classes. I felt as if my time had come and had awoken to what was always with me since childhood. I felt I was doing what I was supposed to be doing. I was on the right path. What a great feeling.

I am still learning. The most fulfilling is when I can assist someone in communicating with a loved one they have lost. Talking to the "dead people" is something I feel honored to do. It is an experience like no other, and always positive and full of love. With our soul, we are connected to Heaven, to the beyond, through our spiritual energy we all have the ability to receive these intuitive gifts by just acknowledging that they are there. With your soul, you can have access to all divine information available. You simply have to accept that it will come to you. I have trained myself to receive the messages and connections. I have faith that the information will come through when it needs to. It is either there or it is not; no guarantees at all. There are times when during a session with someone I might not have a connection. Then there will be times when someone comes with questions about their life path and all that I have is all their "dead people". Sometimes I have a great connection, but it is not from the one the client wanted to hear from. I have faith; I know that what is meant to be will happen. There are times when your loved ones really want to talk to you, but if I am in line at the grocery store and your grandmother wants to say "Hi", I have to ignore her. That is the type of relationship I have with this ability. I do not believe that God wants me to be bombarded with this when there are others here needing me also; like my immediate family. I do allow myself to acknowledge that when one of my loved ones whom has crossed is connecting with me or another family member, I will say "Okay, I know you're here, I accept love from you," and I try to allow that to be enough from me, I look for more signs of confirmation all the time. Most of the time that is all they want to say, "We are here and we send you love." I also give them love back.

Before I start a group or private session, I have nothing but faith to go on. I have to trust and believe in spirit and myself that there will be connections. I have always had connections; I have had faith fulfilled each moment I have been presented with an intentional situation where a reading had to take place. I worry all the time that someone may not come through. That is the human in me, to have doubt, even fear of 'failing' in the client's eyes. Faith carries me always, and I have never been let down. Trusting that this gift is a responsibility allows for the connections to come easily! I don't try and I don't really meditate that much either. I just let it come naturally.

I want to make sure that everyone knows they can be open to receiving messages from Heaven. You can feel the energy. This intuitiveness lies in each of us. If it is part of your life path, then join together with any psychic medium you trust for your own spiritual counseling. Enjoy what is out there in this New Age and charismatic world for both your health and your mind, for your energy and your psyche. It is amazing how the awareness of intuition has developed over the years. There are many great mediums, and many that are not. We should always be intuitive ourselves when seeking a psychic medium. This is what I pray before I sit with someone. I take the control into my own energy and connect to the beyond before I connect to the psychic medium, who is just a human like me.

Dear God,

On this path I am living I find the resources to discover the inner purposes out of my reach at this moment in time.

I humbly seek guidance through you and from you.

I ask that you enlighten the human being that I am going to have faith in with all the impressions you wish me to know and learn, discover and accept, acknowledge and inspire to, which are meant for my path. Have the grace to empower this beautiful human being with the information that I seek to help advance my life and bring me closer to you. Allow them to feel your grace as you connect to the essence of our lives.

Amen.

CHAPTER 4

It's a Job

Them: "Hello Rebecca, nice to meet you. What do you do for work?" Me: "I talk to dead people."

A psychic medium's job: To align you and awaken you, bringing you closer to love; to bring you messages from spirits beyond; to bring you faith and hope for your life; to help you learn how to truly manifest into your life what is perfectly intended to bring you harmony on your path.

To offer this work involves a series of job-related duties. How can you be considered a respected and trusted practitioner? You have to conduct yourself as a business as well as taking the gift and abilities seriously. You make this your life choice, but in turn it requires your time and effort, attention and more. I, too, pay taxes; most psychic mediums do as we earn income for our services. I am a registered business in my home town. I'll never forget the day I received a letter telling me they needed to tax me on my desk, chair, pens and pencils. I was shocked but it was a wake up call to my profession as a working business. Money is needed to survive in today's economy. I have responsibilities to take care of just like everyone else. Part of the job is to keep track of that business end.

Taking time into consideration, I had to make it clear that my business is defined. Seeing how my appointments are guided for my clients, I had to make a lot of choices about what I offered. I also wanted to make sure I was offering what I could deliver. I had to consider dates, times and availability while considering my family responsibilities as well. This balance of time needed to be set into a calendar. You should see the calendar in my home, daily upkeep; it is a large desk calendar that we put up on the wall! In addition, it required a space or location to hold the session in; meaning rental fees, insurance and occasionally advertising.

My services needed to match what I felt comfortable doing as well as how my experience worked for me. Being able to communicate with the spiritual realm as a medium and being intuitive into one's life energy and soul as a psychic, made that title appropriate. Knowing how spirit has control of each session, I expect both of these attributes to appear during a session. Although I do not have control of who appears to whom, I do consider myself able to conduct sessions according to client's preference.

I say it is like I am the switchboard. I do not have the control to answer the phone, but spirit has control to put me on speaker phone. Sometimes there will be a few lines open at once. This is an overload to my senses and receiving. I just tell my "dead people" that they need to slow down and take a moment to organize for me. I look at the spirits of our loved ones as the same soul energy they were when there were "here" in body. We keep our free will! It is an awesome energy that is us and when your loved ones come through they may be quiet and call my line to talk to you or they may be loud and scream into the speakerphone connection, all full of love and electricity. They control the readings, we are there to receive.

Offering you a psychic reading: A psychic reading is a way for a psychic medium to give time to someone with the intention to give them all intuitive impressions. That information will guide them on their path; heal blocks from that path while helping them move forward with more clarity and confirmation toward the direction to go next on that very life path. The most common psychic topics: Past, Present and Future, Physical, Social, Emotional, Mental and Spiritual. Money, Love, Marriage, Dating, Vacation, Visiting, Travel, Moving, Real Estate, Employment, Home, Environments, Financial Investments, Friendships, Health, Prosperity, Forgiveness, Family, Soul Mates Job, Relationships, Transportation, Purchases, Arguments, Religion, Spiritual Growth, Children, Decision Making, Education and Trust PLUS whatever else there is that you could think of. Any aspect of life and MORE!

Where a psychic reading is a knowing through the gift of wisdom there is the confirmation that a psychic does indeed read the energy of the person. I feel energy that is filled with information, and trust that all psychic information I receive is being revealed to me with open willingness and purpose through that client's soul. The soul speaks through us. When I am channeling, receiving information from beyond that inner soul of that person, the soul connection reaches out from their body and embraces more information from beyond for me to receive. This information is from beyond our human body and the energy field that surrounds us. It is more direct and powerful.

Offering you Channeling: A process of receiving information through direct focus and understanding from angels, archangels, ascended masters, spirit guides and your higher self spirit. All of these angels and guides speak directly through me for you. There are messages from your soul, your inner child and your heart. Profound connections can be made to Jesus, His brothers, the saints, archetypes and prophets. The best part of this is that when I am channeling, I am not sure who it is at all, just that I know it is an entity which is under God and I am OK connect. The vibration will start in my lips and move through my mouth. I can hear what I am saying and I have control to interrupt myself, but I am not speaking and when I am done, I do not remember what I have said. It is usually a few short moments, maybe just five minutes of talking. I usually find it is words which come directly through me to hit the heart of the person I am speaking to, and to them the words hit their soul with direct confirmation of what there need on this path currently is. Something I say that "Rebecca Anne" probably would not be able to say. So it comes and with it, I have faith and trust.

Offering Mediumship: The most profound connections I have are the souls of our loved ones that cross. There is no better feeling than to have the dead speak to the living. The love is an energy better then any drug, food, song; anything! The physical euphoria I feel when the souls speak to me is sometimes overwhelming. I never know what they are going to say, or how it is going to come across and be accepted. It is a shock for me to hear the validation as much as it is a shock to the person receiving the message to be able to say "yes". We love them, as we are human and miss them. This connection through mediumship, which is channeling, touches my heart the most.

When all is said and done, this job is a job. It is one with responsibility and ethics. It is sometimes tiring to the mind and exhausting to the body. As with all jobs, it is one that you must love to do to achieve the highest good from the experiences. Going full-time requires a reputation to be considered, alongside the rest of the responsibilities. It is a perfect, loving, fulfilling job.

CHAPTER 5

Myth: Psychic Mediums Are Just For Paranormal Shows to Deal with Hauntings

I can not say for sure, as I am not crossed over, what exactly is happening when there are souls that linger here on earth with us within our timeline. They do not age, they just connect. I know that when I cross over, I am not planning to 'dwell' in my house and haunt someone. I plan to be in a million places at once, enjoying the timeless moments of love and joy, humor, hugs from those I reconnect with and more. There may be many stories that are scary and confusing, but they are alongside some loving and persistent stories of souls that just want to keep their energy close to the earth. Both of these situations are paranormal in nature. I have had many sessions that involved a reading of a specific location such as a home, office or land. These are definite 'paranormal investigations' that I was involving myself in through general readings to actual cases. As a psychic you have the ability to tune into the energy. I wanted to add this information into this book because there should not always a bad feeling attached to having someone haunt, or dwell, within your space. I have one story I want to connect this to that I share below. I leave this in your hands to consider how you feel. I know how it made me feel while I was channeling.

This photo above has the possible spiritual manifestation of the figure of a little girl about age nine. The photo was taken with a digital camera at 10:00 a.m., with the sun directly behind us. This shadow appears to have her holding a cloak around her head and has a hand holding it tight under her chin. There is a bright line of light above her forehead. Other areas of the photo were also blurred for no reason. Below is the story behind the photo.

CHAPTER 6

Connecting With the Spirit of a Little Girl

"On October 9th in 2002, I was in Lisa's backyard. Lisa is a great friend of mine who is a High Wiccan Priestess. I had already told her there was a presence of a little girl. I was hoping to confirm that. I did. As I entered the woods line, near the old foundation made of rocks, I felt a little girl right away. I thought this was a serious situation. As I wandered around telling the story that I was feeling and hearing from this little girl, Gerri Karamesinis and Jay Stock were snapping pictures of me storytelling and connecting. First, I knew that there was a little girl. I felt that she was alone and had been left that way. I felt that there was a stone fence around a perimeter that this little girl stayed in. She knows that Lisa lit candles in her backyard and that brought this girl to her. She was in clothes resembling the early 1800's. These clothes were super big on her. She told me that she went to a house that was in the back of the extended yard. This other little house was a place where she admitted to stealing items; clothes, toys and maybe food. Alone for a few years, she managed to survive on her own until she brought me to where she laid her head and died, at the age of nine. She lay down her head upon other graves of the dead. Being left alone at such a young age, I do not think that she understood about mourning death. It was not explained to her. She had a goat. This goat was her friend. She would drink the warm goat's milk and she seemed to tell me that she would stuff her oversized dress with the goat fur to keep her warm also. I felt that her home was destroyed, possibly by fire. I felt that it was not her fault either. Now, I felt that she was telling me a sound. Not that she could speak well; it was almost as if she did not have the ability to communicate verbally. The only sound I could understand her say was "Pow. Pow." This seemed to represent to her what had happened to the men who took care of her. They left due to the "Pows"! These might have been gunfire. I felt like there was no mother to be found. Maybe that she did not ever know her mother. I had more of a male presence. They seemed to be uncles or brothers; three of them total. This nine-year-old girl was abandoned, whether it was the fault of the men, or the tragedy of a close battle. She managed to live off the land for a few years.

I knew she had a strong energy that could present itself. I asked Lisa if there was a wind back there on a flat and windless day. Her answer was "always." This was the energy of the girl taking her strolls through this land that Lisa's house is on. Lisa also told me that old and broken toys often seem to unbury themselves on a small path near the foundation. These toys were broken and from different generations. I felt the toys in my hands. They seemed to become unburied from a sort of picnic basket. I felt that, even though this girl did not own these toys, she did use that energy of hers to unearth the toys. I did mention that I did not think that she was very smart. I also felt that she was a bit timid and scared at times. I thought that if she were smarter I would be able to communicate with her better. She did not leave the areas that she knew. This area is not more than two acres. Down behind the foundation I felt that there was a dip or gully that would be filled with water. At some point, this was a gravesite. This fact did not disturb the girl, as it just seemed normal. There was no one around her at all. She seemed to be unable to function properly for some reason, resulting in her death also. She went to this spot of death and died there herself, leaving her spirit to arise and continue there. I offered her the help to leave, and prayed that someone would help her go. Will she? We don't know if or when.

Later on in the day, four of us at Lisa's set up and prepared to call on a spirit to come and take this girl to Heaven. We asked that God let someone who knows her and loves her have the ability to remove this little girl from this land where she was abandoned and let her go join her family in Heaven. The energy that came upon us during the ceremony rocked the tall candlesticks behind us and made the flame on the candles tilt with the wind that was present in the room. Feeling the spirit come and get her was awesome. Everyone in the room felt and knew our prayers and questions were getting attention. A miracle? Success is what I was hoping for; that there would be a transition, if that was what God intended for her.

Here is the clincher. In the evening when the shoot was over, I came home tired and drained. Gerri, who had taken digital pictures, was downloading them on her computer and showing them to her assistant and Jay. When they got to the ones that were taken while I was reading the spirit of the girl in the back yard, there was one that was very special. The silhouette of the girl's head was right there on my body. The apparition just seemed to be attached to my side from my breast to my mid-stomach. The angle of the light and the shadow or illusion that it caused was unnatural for the camera. It was something that was not seen with the human eye at the time the pictures were taken. Was it that the little girl was with me as she spoke through me? Was I holding her to me? She was there and that I believe! With her face seeming to be distorted from some illness maybe? With her hand holding a cloak on her head? You decide for yourself."

I do believe that souls stay around; they come and go. I do also believe that sometimes they do not want to go up to Heaven; they do not want to leave their past. Most do not understand that they can go and that might even make them edgy. However, each time I come across a lingering soul, I always ask for the light of God and the Heavens to open up wide so they can see and choose to go or stay. Sometimes they stay. It is not up to us as humans to make that choice for them. The gift of free will does not leave our soul when we die; it is a part of our soul.

CHAPTER 7

How to Understand the Negative Aspects and Opinions of the Work a Psychic Medium Does

More often than not, psychic mediumship is associated with evil spirits. It is not uncommon for those who are not aware of what the job entails to believe there is an association to Satan and bad curses, etc. Here is one perspective I can share. Be yourself, know your resources, and don't contradict yourself. I often find issues with some overly developed modalities. If you are going to take a class, then do your research. I would not go to an angel class if the teacher did not believe in the devil. This may sound weird, but how can one reference the angels of God and disregard the opposition? The devil is also known as the 'angel of light' in the stories through history.

Here is a brief history of the 'concept' of Satan. I will only discuss this briefly due to the fact that I believe in my soul there should be little to no acknowledgements made of the evil end of things. Why? I believe that whatever you bring your attention to is drawn to you and that is not something I want to have drawn to anyone, anywhere, in any place at any time!

I do, however, feel there is great power when we acknowledge something! To acknowledge brings the opportunity to accept or deny. This is a way to bring discernment into your judgment of situations. With that being said, there are a few perspectives to consider. Within Christianity, it states in the Bible that Satan was known as the guardian of the first humans who became one of God's most trusted angels. He rebelled against God because he thought himself a better king.

From an Islamic point of view, God is seen to have created the angels and the djinns. Angels were formed from bright light and were sent to Heaven and the djinns were created from smokeless fire and sent to earth. Then God made Adam and Eve. IZAZIL (Satan) was the leader of an arm of djinns, and lead an army and was successful in the pursuit. The angels in Heaven asked God to promote Satan from earth to a place called the Seventh Sky in Heaven. Once there, he was ordered along with the angels to bow down in front of Adam and Eve, and IZAZIL did not. God then changed his name to Satan and kicked him out of Heaven. I am aware of many more stories and theories.

Whether Satan is real or not, it is just the negativity that we use to try to explain away malevolence. We do this by making excuses for humanity and laying these excuses upon evil. It is there at times and to acknowledge it allows you to reject it. No psychic medium should delve into the realm of evil for information or channeled intuitive impressions. That would be working without discernment. I think it is unhealthy and crazy too! I focus the reality of the afterlife and the positive that comes with that. Negative or evil spirits are not a resource considered to be purposeful when considering the openness of your free will when receiving. In fact, it could be dangerous. Only focusing on the highest good in all situations is an idea, but is that reality? We have to acknowledge to be able to discern and react with honest acceptance of each situation. The reality is we can all do this. We can all connect, but to do this for others or for work, we must be sure that the mental and psychological strengths are there as well as the intuitive abilities.

CHAPTER 8

Living As a Psychic Medium: A Life Choice Involving Acceptance

B y no means did I ever think I would be a psychic medium when I grew up. I thought I would be a psychologist or child therapist. However, it was overwhelming how I always knew there was something more. At every turn there were wake-up calls to what these gifts and abilities were. I would often prove myself correct on thoughts, dreams, ideas and impressions. I knew that I was psychic. To take that information and go out into the world was another thing. I have to say I am very lucky. I have an extremely supportive network of family and friends; something that you generally need in life. To go forward and tell family and friends what you can do is a huge step; you will find that they will either say "I will pray for your soul" or "Can I have a reading?" It is fine either way. If they are not comfortable, it is not my choice to change their minds or get them to understand. It is not my job to force anyone to accept something with which they are not comfortable.

Often the unknown of the profession makes people scared. That fear of the unknown puts many on the defense. That is the way society has treated this metaphysical area. Fortunetellers at the old fairgrounds are great examples; usually you see them in horror movies. Consider how the prophets felt at their time. The past was not kind to those who would insist that God was speaking to them or through them for others. In Exodus, we can read about how Moses did not want to lead the people to the Promised Land, but with his faith he persevered as a prophet and was guided by God each step of the way with miraculous experiences.

The life choice to accept psychic mediumship does not make you any different than the rest of the humans on this earth. You will not all of a sudden have some special status. Psychic mediums have the ups and downs which life gives us all. We have the kids to care for; we are divorced and remarried. Basically, we are not immune to what the world hands each of us. I have experienced birth and death; I have lost jobs and fallen short financially. I do not have special treatment from above. I still have to be careful not to get into accidents; I have to discern who comes into my life; and I have in-laws to love and friends to help. I lean on friends to help me and I am just living life like the rest of humankind. This life choice to have a job which deals with accepting the messages that come from Heaven does not make me immune to the path and plan which God has for me. I find more often than not that I am aligned in perfection to the places and people that I meet. Is that because I am intuitive? God blesses me that much? I believe I am just aware of the intuitive paths and experiences along with the psychic phenomena which is present always. I can tap into that and it is useful! I just choose to accept with understanding and acknowledgement that there is, indeed, more to life then just being here on earth. We all should take that to our hearts and believe and know it as truth. There is a beyond to which we can all connect!

What to Do With This Gift?

I have the gift of intuition, the gift of knowing, and the gift to have and bear this ability while in this human body. Yes, it is a gift. I will not deny that it is also an ability which everyone has, that has been debated over and over. However, the truth is that God gave this gift to each of us as our souls came into body. We have always had this connection to the beyond. This can be seen when we set a goal for ourselves and reach it. We have paths: the strong connection to information about our paths is within us. This gift brings forth into our lives and draws to us what we need to manifest the most to advance here on earth. It is one step in bringing experiences to our soul purposes. This gift can show itself in a sign, a letter, a friend; any kind of connection we make with all parts of our lives. Soul communication and interaction are signs in themselves more than could be explained. It is all with purpose and that purpose is constantly being made aware to us in manifested ways.

This gift -- to be able to see what is coming -- understanding the reasons for the past, and to connect with all present situations with clear understanding has always been within each of us. At this point, it is a matter of acknowledging and accepting while attuning your awareness to this fact. This gift is special and given to us without limits, just as we have free will here on earth to experience and love, to have opinions and desires. This gift is also ours to choose to use or to be aware of its existence. It is possible that there are people who are supposed to use these gifts they have to be intuitive as a job, as a life's mission; and there are those who are not pushed to involve their gifts in others lives, but to keep this information to themselves to work with and to accept. Either way is fine. In fact, I believe there are so many reasons and ways to connect with your intuition that one book could not explain it all. There is something special about being intuitively aware in your own life in a personal way. I have that connection as well and nurture it daily. There are also those who know that they are not connected to their gift for a variety of reasons and that would be why a psychic medium might benefit them. That is why psychic mediums are there working, making their gift available to heal, advance, and renew their soul's path in life. I have gone to see a psychic medium for readings, direction, for connections to loved ones that have crossed, as well as for idle curiosity toward a future path. There is a spiritual growth that can happen when you reach out for it.

Enlightenment comes when this gift is present either on a personal level or when it is joined with someone who is connected to Spirit as a way to help others. There is responsibility with this gift not to abuse it, not to take advantage of others and to share the truth for each individual which comes to those who have it. If you have a gift and it is used with positive intention, there will be accuracy. To have such accuracy explains how powerful of a connection it is to go with the pure line from your inner soul to the beyond.

CHAPTER 9

The Ability — In Terms and Definition

B eyond this being a gift, it is an ability that must in some way be connected to the human body. As a psychic medium, people often ask me if I can teach them how to do this. Can I teach you? Yes, I know I can. Should I teach you? That may be, but I do not have a specific 'how to' manual and no process I 'teach' will completely give you the grace and ability, discernment and energy to do what I do! Faith is all you need to do what I do; faith and a 'just do it' attitude. We can all connect to this gift as an active ability within our daily lives. It is our right as a human body which contains this soul to be able to connect with God. In doing so, there are many ways which we can physically use our mind to connect to that information our soul is receiving.

We are all human and have this ability naturally. When I say this, it is a very open-ended statement. There are many techniques, modalities and processes I have learned. I was curious. I knew God so from there, I had quite the religious foundation but I wanted more understanding. I still want more understanding. Back 18 plus years ago, the library was the only place I could find information to satisfy my curiosity. Times have changed a lot in the course of a few years. There are now degrees available in parapsychology, metaphysical studies and more. There are 1000's of books on every New Age subject, with more on the way. I believe the access to information has expanded through the Internet. Holistic centers are worldwide with a rotating and expanding awareness for all who explore what is being offered. Even Oprah Winfrey has offered information to the general public, resulting in an opening up of awareness in society. If you talk to any teenagers, they know TV shows like "That's So Raven" and "Wizards of Waverly Place", Disney shows which depict the afterlife and psychic impressions in each show!

Here I will describe, in my own brief definitions, a list of general 'abilities' I have and use. Also listed are some common terms I have heard and come across, which people associate to this metaphysical idea of psychic mediumship. I am not trying to list all words; there are many missing. Synchronicity always brings us down paths to learn something new. Some of these abilities listed below I have gone to school or classes to learn; in others I have even been certified. Some are abilities I have discovered I had naturally, while others I worked hard to achieve proficiency in through research and study. As you read this list below, notice how many connections you have to the words. Do you feel how you can understand these definitions in an acknowledging way or an accepting way? As a human, we all are connected to each other and Spirit. In turn, we are all connected to the intuitive, psychic, spiritual intuition that we own through our soul connections. These terms are stated as a way to introduce and awaken those gifts you already have an ability to achieve.

Psi – A general term used for all types of psychic phenomena.

Paranormal – Psychic or mental experiences considered outside the range of something normal, including all things beyond the ordinary or expected; something that cannot be defined in normal terms.

Parapsychology – A branch of psychology that researches and investigates Psi, (psychic phenomena)

Psyche – The human soul; the mind.

Occult – Hidden, concealed, secret, cryptic, unable to be understood fully, not within human comprehension; mysterious. Occultism is the belief in occult forces and powers.

Remote Viewing – The ability to use the mind's eye to see a person, place or thing situated in a different location. This location is beyond the physical area of the one remote viewing. This ability reveals people and actions taking place in this other location.

Creative Visualization – The process to bring into your life a creation of your visual image through an expression of imagination and desire. This produces the idea that the outcome will be what is visualized; this is often done through prayer and meditation.

Extrasensory Perception or ESP – Scientific term for perception without use of the known human senses (touch, taste, smell, hear, sight) also known as the sixth sense. The scientific term is 1 'biocommunication'. BACKSTER, C. (2003), Primary Perception: Biocommunication with

Plants, Living Foods, and Human Cells. California, White Rose Millennium Press.

Precognition – Perceiving the future. Cognition is attaining the knowledge and ideas and then perceiving them. Precognition is knowing or perceiving something 'beforehand.'

Retro cognition – 'Seeing' intuitively an occasion that took place before the current time.

Telepathy or Mental Telepathy – Communication to mind from mind. Greek word 'tele' means 'far off, at a distance.' The word 'telephone' means 'speaking at a distance.' The Greek word 'pathos' means 'experience or emotion.' Mental Telepathy is therefore, 'to experience something at a distance through mental communication rather than by physical means.'

Clairvoyance –Thoughts received to your awareness from an unknown resource. A knowing of what can not be seen; having the meaning and understanding without previous exposure.

Clairaudience - To be able to hear a sound from your mind, beyond time and space.

Clairempathy – A person who feels the emotional attachments from other people, places or things with which they are energetically connected.

Clairscent – To smell the thought from your mind of a significant fragrance not present in the physical environment, while receiving that essence.

Akashic Record or Universal Consciousness – A place believed to be the holder of all; meaning that as the oneness of all energy is connecting us, we are able to tap into the energy as it is cosmically and quantumly part of our human energy field.

Psychometry – A process of connecting to the energy around an object while being open to accepting impressions and feelings. Reading what the energy was or is connected to that has been absorbed into the item. Dr. J. R. Buchanan in 1842 Manual of Psychometry (Boston, 1889)

Aura – Your body has an energy field. This energy holds all information as in mental, physical, emotional and past and present energetic influences to and from you. This aura is a reflection of what is inside you, as well as a resource to receive from the outside.

Chakra – Points of connection at which energy flows within your body, all having specific meaning and purpose within your body which coincides with your harmonious states. There are seven chakras most commonly associated to center points up the middle of the body.

Manifestation – The process by which you take notice and action to attain something you want be it mental, material, physical, spiritual or likewise, with full intension of receiving it.

Materialization – Through Spirit the power to manifest to be seen with physical eyes.

Prophecy – Receiving information about the future.

Dowsing – Ancient technique to finding water.

Trance/Channeling – A medium receives a message, vision or dream through Spirit through their body.

Healing – The ability to heal the physical body.

Spiritual Communication Through a Medium – Discernment of Spirits in Biblical terms.

Automatic Writing – A trademark for my readings is a written form of intuitive information. I write while I am sitting with you. There will always be a piece of paper which I use to write down the messages and insight I receive. This free writing produces detailed information which might not be verbalized during the reading. This is a reference for you to take home with you to remember your reading.

Counseling & Therapy – Each and very reading involves insight and clarity into the personal aspects of one's life. It is a therapeutic and inspirational session. I have the education and background in psychology to know and understand life situations in an objective and individual way. I often refer to the coping skills and proactive methods I have learned to move your life in a positive direction.

Past Life Stories – Sometimes I am able to see important and significant issues that seem to relate to a different time or era. These situations can relate to any and all aspects of your life.

Visualization – Sometimes it is important to use visualization to move ahead on your spiritual path. This involves breathing and relaxing with your eyes closed, while focusing on God and receiving information through imagination.

Chapter 10

Looking at Mediumship and Discernment of Spirits

A s a medium, I am able to communicate directly to the souls of our loved ones who have died. With this gift comes the responsibility to be able to discern what information is coming through and from whom. Pure and positive knowledge should always be received through the highest good to us. The negative information, if at all, should be discerned with caution and always result in the higher good for everyone.

What specifically is this 'Discernment of Spirits'? It is a statement made in the Bible (1 Corinthians 12:10) which describes one of the many gifts the Holy Spirit gives us. Discernment is partly described as being able to accept and interpret all information, the good and the bad. This is an inner-conscious connection to the 'just knowing' if someone or something, such as a thought or concept, is right or wrong. One can discern what is true and what is not. There are good spirits and bad energies; because of this it is important to be able to have this ability when communicating with the spiritual realm. It is the truthfulness through discernment that I receive when I talk to the dead. This gift is my way to protect myself from the evil and false information which could come through. I believe that I have two very large guardian angels behind me using their wings to help filter the information for me. I do not read negative or false information, nor do I receive information about illness or death. This discerning happens through the energy involved in the connection before I communicate with the spirit. I do not hold back on anything I receive. Whether it makes sense at the moment or not, I cannot lie about what I receive; I just play the role of the messenger.

Trying to describe the actual process of communication? I must say that it is always important to remember we are all human and the actual act of communication with another realm is quite unexplainable. There are a lot of theories, possibilities and explanations. For myself, I just believe that it is true. I know it is there and I acknowledge that it is a gift for me to share. I have no true answer to how it 'really' happens. Physically, I feel high vibrational energy connecting to my body. My energy level rises and sometimes I have to stand up or move around to gain focus. It is a good feeling that often comes on suddenly. I frequently use my ability to channel while writing to concentrate on the information as it comes. This is how I know that someone is connecting to me. I can ignore this feeling and it will go away or I bring focus to my mind so I can receive the messages coming through. I am not in a trance; I am not doing a séance. I am completely awake and fully aware of what is happening.

I can then see with my mind's eye the location from where the information is coming. I sense the information in many ways such as sight, sound and smell, and relay it as best I can for the person for whom the information is meant. This is all happening with the help of the Holy Spirit to guide me to understand and interpret the connection fully. Because there is no time in Heaven, the spirit has no boundaries to the impressions or information that I receive. Meaning the person may appear old, young, loud or quiet, shy or of any other temperament or description to confirm that it is them. A few commonalities seen with each connection is good health, happiness and an outpouring of love.

It is important to consider there is some connection to the way that they meet with me; a pattern which matches many other mediums' techniques. When someone comes through, the mothers and family are on your right side, fathers and family are on the left. The energy around us all is in motion and very vibrational. (This is a great time for spirit photography; snapping many pictures in a row to catch the orbs left in the energy field.) Remember, where they are has no concept of time, so there is a connection with our world that does not follow the laws of conversations. Information is implanted, not a memory to recall, and it comes instantaneously and repetitively. Interpretation can be shady at times or even confusing, as I am still in my human body with a human way to understand. The Holy Spirit allows my body's vibrational field to accept the information and to connect to my spirit. It is quite the combination of faith and science. I am able to receive, interpret and share. Is it quantum physics, energy, molecules or is it something more mystical? I believe it to be a beautiful and spiritually fulfilling supernatural and miraculous experience.

CHAPTER 11

Truly Receiving the Information: How the Connection Can Happen Through a Psychic Medium

There is a reality to receiving this information. It does happen. If you give your soul awareness more attention by focusing, you will receive. I often just bend my head a little as to 'listen' better and allow the energy to try to come right into my ears. It is amazing when I actually 'hear' someone giving me information. It could be a flash of sound or a light script of words, but it is still received. It is a focus on the moment when you are specifically looking to accept the information. It is there for you to pull it in instead of just 'catching' it.

In my mind, these thoughts come from the unknown. There are no known scientific reasons for how or why thoughts can be confirmed as facts coming from someone who has no previous knowledge of the situations. Ninety percent of the time I receive this kind of information when I am trying to. This does not always take much effort. The more you open up to receive information about someone, something or someplace, the easier it becomes to gather it.

This is a good example of how it is ability and should be treated as such. Quite frankly, if I was to look at or focus on one person or thing for too long, I tend to automatically pick up information relating to them. This information can sometimes be confirmed. When I am working with someone, the confirmation for this information is usually immediate. It is often necessary to receive one part of information with confirmation so that a deeper validation can come to the situation. For example when you call a friend at the same time they were calling you, your thoughts were out there as were your friend's. Your energies connected thoroughly. How about when you decide, last second, to take the back roads instead of the highway? Your thoughts in turn interpret your actions and you find out later there was a big crash. What were your senses gathering? Intuition of what your energies were going to experience. Call it gut instinct, luck or intuition, it is all the same.

This sensing of information comes into one's aura, their physical body, their actual being. There is the sixth sense to be able to read this information and then some. One must interpret the information through the other five senses, making it easier to understand and pass on. I can read energies which are to come, but often I first interpret what is present. What is currently happening can be easier to read. Knowing and confirming what is real and happening now helps to see where it will go next if it keeps on the same path. This allows you to be open to see other possible paths also.

Using tarot cards is using your sense of seeing as well. You see the cards and use them to interpret in your mind's eye what you are really seeing or feeling about that person or situation. Regardless of how you were to interpret each card, the thoughts are always the most important. God talks to us in many ways, through many tools and resources. He uses what is perfect for us to receive from in this lifetime.

I may read in your energy the smell of pipe tobacco and I may see a Florida coast. These senses come at the same time, only to be confirmed as a visitor from Florida who smokes a pipe is staying with them. It is very important to be aware of what you see, saying everything you feel as fast as you can. If I feel sand or dirt on my hands, I focus on the feeling and embrace why I feel that. It may be that sand is going to be an important key word to understanding whatever is to come. Trusting my feelings, first-sense reactions are the key to a satisfying session. There are so many aspects of life to be considered that you have to be open to whatever comes. The feeling of sand on your hands may confirm for the person that they will indeed be going to Florida themselves to bring the visitor back home. This information may now be confirming the idea of their trip for them. It is not how I feel about what impressions I receive, but it is how the person I am with interprets what I say.

I always work within white light and look for positive intuitions. I speak lightly when negative thoughts come. I focus on purpose of the connections through my soul and my clients. When this all began for me the negative energy was the easiest to read. I look past that and know that generally people learn from their pasts. When you have had a negative experience in your life, it makes you who you are and it becomes a part of you. The life you live is full of ups and downs. Seeing into the down part only helps me to move into where you are now and how you will move forward even more. I find that being a realist, being aware of the real world and speaking in down-to-earth conversations with clients is what they want. They want truth, core impressions and exactly what is coming is exactly what is meant to be shared.

When reading spirit, the more people there are involved, the more clarification I have to put on each. Psychicly I will connect personality traits as well. I am known to take on the mannerisms of the dead like they were dancing in my body. The more people involved, the more information needs to be spoken and clarified so intuitively I can move deeper into the importance of the matter. I feel it is a waste of your time if I just reference the surface of a situation. I want to get to the point. Don't we all want to find the center of each situation so we can see it clearly? There is a reason for everything and I love to help, heal and enlighten anyone even remotely interested in sharing an experience of a session with me. The greatest gifts are when I can let someone know when a loved one is standing by them, or when a fantastic opportunity awaits them.

Chapter 12

Lots of Responsibility

I also have to accept all of the other responsibilities which fall in line with calling myself a psychic medium. One has to have ethics and take this profession as a gift, which is to be shared. It is a reality when making this choice. It is a job outside the norm of what we consider to be everyday life. I know that there is a reason to do this work in this lifetime, but I have often thought about how split my life is. There are days when I don't feel like I have any gifts or abilities at all! Days when the dishes are piled high, the relative's birthday party is at noon and responsibilities are listed on the refrigerator. I still worry at times before sessions that I might not be able to deliver the communication from spirits which my clients have come to hear. Can you imagine how scary that is? I don't know if all intuitives feel that, but I am sure there are moments for all of us when we are just not sure of the outcome of a situation into which we are putting our faith. This job for me is a life choice that I am willing to share with everyone. Having to live with this Heavenly connection and still live within the social environment of my life can be a challenge and a blessing.

I have children. This leads me to take the abilities I have and suppress them, so as to not cause issues within my children's lives. It is not always cool for a young child to have to deal with the fact that people are judgmental. Outsiders and insiders in my life can be judgmental and I have to take that with stride. I have to discern who to let know what I do for a living and who to tell that I am a homemaker (my other job). I embrace and accept this responsibility with great discernment however I do not hide it when it's put on the line. This ability does not have a good hiding place. I can remember how hard it was to keep this work outside of the social environment of my oldest daughter's school parent and teacher association. She would insist that I not tell anyone what I do for work because she did not want to have the kids start to ask her for readings too. That was not her idea of being accepted. Again, there is a social responsibility to not make someone uncomfortable while you are trying at the same time to be honest and responsible when dealing with this gift.

CHAPTER 13

How Could This Gift To Connect With God Be A Burden?

When speaking in front of an audience which is waiting with bated-breath for me to start channeling the loved ones in the room, I get filled with a compassion and love. I look over a crowd of loving humans, all there praying and asking their loved ones to be the stronger energy and come through me. I have heard participants of a group talking before I went on. "I know my relative will come. They promised me they would." I mention this because the loving promise which they felt 'was' the fulfillment. They did come to you, they did tell you that. Indeed they are there with you. We interpret our inner desires as facts. The burden of not connecting with someone lays heavy on my heart as well. Even though I know it is out of my control, I still feel empathetic. I have also had callers on the line waiting to connect with me for readings on the radio. One told me that I was unfair to not take his call, as he was waiting for 45 minutes. He had put the intention 'out there' to manifest that he wanted a reading so he felt that he deserved it, as it was his intention to take the action to call in, making it a force from his soul to feel he was going to get connected. When his call was not answered for whatever reason, he was angry and felt that his intention was purposely ignored by me. I don't have control over where spirit comes through, but for some reason this man felt that I did. I do not have control of spirit, nor does that man have control over what he truly manifests.

My burden in a room full of people waiting for me to come to them is this: I cannot connect with everyone. I am human and I can only go for so long. I cannot control who comes in for whom. I have come to a full awareness of that and find peace in the fact that I am going to do my best and with faith and trust, I will connect where I should. Being human again, I leave each group with a sense of sadness, a heavy heart for those who I do not connect for. It is a part of this work. I cry; I want to read for everyone! I just do my best to read for as many as I can and have faith in the knowing that those who do not get a personal connection receive the energy and love from heaven also! As a goal, if I read a room of 500, and read only 20, I feel that I have touched the heart of the other 480 people also.

It is not always a burden but it sure can be hard at times. At some point, one who is a psychic medium must admit that it has awoken them enough to know this is a responsibility; something that has to be shared, expressed, and used for the higher good of all society. This burden is one that I feel is heavy at times, but never impossible. There are so many people who want and need insight, intuitive healing, spiritual connections to heal grief and wounds within. Beyond the obvious expressions of who I am and what I do, there is the need to explain and convince. Not that this is necessary, but to touch as many people as possible it is necessary to explain myself to help open others up. I find myself explaining over and over again. This is okay. I know it is needed and I encourage all intuitives to keep explaining and if you don't understand, keep asking. Be aware there is no room for skepticism, no need for animosity, and no fear associated to this at all. Opening others up, awakening their souls to the energy around them is the responsibility that at times can be hard.

I remember one time I was at a gathering where we were doing cold readings for members of a group of over 100 people. This beautiful woman grabbed me, pulling on my arm. She wanted me to come to her next to give her a spirit connection. Now, I am spirit-guided so the soul that comes through is not up to me. I often wish it were up to me. This woman wanted to hear from her mom and sisters, not her husband who died and left her feeling abandoned and angry! However, of course the husband's energy wants to come through; wants to repair that lingering feeling; repair his wife's emotional standing so he is the only soul I have for her. That burden is there to perform as this woman looks at me, not as a human being, but as a performer who can produce results. There is the explanation; there is that expression of my responsibility as the channel, as the medium, instead of the one in control. I can not fake it and will not lie to you. No medium should, but they do. My heart hangs so heavy for those who do not get the connections they need. I have faith and trust that when the time is right, they will!

CHAPTER 14

A Story: One Answer from God and One Psychic Reading in New York

In a fit of grief over the loss of a loved one, I took an opportunity to do some volunteer work in New York which brought me directly to the hometown of the loved one I had lost. This visit I handled privately and I did not want any of the family members connected to this loved one to know I was there. I traveled four hours in the rain to arrive tired, cold, confused and with a need for a bathroom. This destination was a harbor park where there was a bench placed as a memorial for this loved one I was grieving. My idea was to go sit on this bench, gather my sorrow, bond with the situation and do some healing on myself. All this was action I was taking to connect with that soul, just as I tell my clients to do. I was so unsatisfied with my situation and the path it was taking, due to the fact that I was basically within the norm of the grief process.

At that moment I wanted a reading! I wanted someone to connect for me to this loved one's pure soul so I could embrace the reality and hear their message with human clarity. Up the Main Street of this town, beyond the harbor park area, were a series of shops and restaurants. I started up this road to find food, a place to freshen up, and settle after the drive. The sidewalks were barren but the stores were open. I wondered into a garden trinket store and said to myself in a small whisper, "God, please give me someone to tell my story to." As I walked out the door of that shop I noticed across the street this cute little house which was out of character for the rest of the street. There were two businesses sharing the home. On the left, a jewelry store and on the right was a psychic medium! Thank my lucky stars, the answer to my very prayer. I walked (skipped really) across the street and saw that she was with a client, so went into the other half of the house. These two locations shared a porch.

This fancy and small jewelry store was run by this beautiful curly-haired lady, who welcomed me in and allowed me to use her bathroom. She smiled at my desire to see the psychic and mentioned I could sit and wait on the porch. I instantly loved this woman. As I sat outside waiting for the psychic to be free of her current client, this woman from the jewelry store came to sit next to me on a bench out front. Her words to me at that moment will stay with me forever, as a reminder of how God's intuitive energy and intentions are perfect. She said, "Soooooo," with a long and interested sigh, "Tell me your story." Short of quoting my very thought and prayer to God, she opened in my heart the idea that perfection lay within my visit to New York. I told her my story; healing pouring out of me with every word carefully so I did not burden her with drama. She was so calm and kind and did not respond with opinion, but guided her question to me with sincerity and love. I even told her how I was a psychic seeking a psychic for that very validation that she had just given me. I wish I could say that was the end of the story but it was not. I continued to wait for the psychic to be free and was hopeful that I would still receive some fulfillment from her messages for me. I was going with an open heart and willingness. I should have, or could have, listened to that inner voice and saved myself a significant amount of money. This psychic was not connected. She was not with God and she did nothing for me except reinforce and teach me to be aware of the manifestation of intuition at all times, as it may randomly come to you without you even noticing. My desire to connect though a psychic medium outweighed the discernment I should have had to stay away from that particular intuitive. I accepted that life lesson. I am still connected to that angel from the jewelry store. I often go back to New York and sit on the bench. I feel solid and connected when I visit the hometown of my loved one.

CHAPTER 15

Ethics: Expanding Morality

I have met my share of psychics and mediums in the past twenty years. Some of them are clearly gifted beyond what I could ever imagine. Some gifted but snobs, others who think they have a gift but just don't have the ability to hear and share. Many who are just charlatans! This line of work requires a significant shift in your life. I find it impossible to lie, hurt someone on purpose, or even have anything but love for everyone, even if someone should be hated. I find that judgment is a human characteristic and like all jobs we judge our counterparts but it is not a good feeling. I find it is important for every psychic medium to contemplate what their ethics are and where they stand. A client can gain a sense of understanding, as well as a level of comfort; if they can see you have a conscious awareness that this line of work needs ethics. Below is a general list of ethics I hold to firmly.

Rebecca Anne's Ethics

1. It is my responsibility to be honest with you. All information I receive for you, whether it is from energy or spirit, I will share with you.

2. As a medium, I will do my best to share with you proof and validation of the spiritual realm.

3. As a psychic, I will provide you with accurate and validating information directly connected to your current life and spiritual path.

4. As a healer, I will always allow the guidance to fill and flow through me to bring healing to all that come in the way which is intended for their body's highest good; through God's direction, as healing is the work of miracles and should be treated as so.

5. I will not impede on your free will nor will I say or do anything that will cause you dismay in any way. I do not read death or serious illness to come. (I believe in miracles.)

6. I will not allow a client to feel as if they are being wronged or cheated in anyway. There are times when I can be incorrect, as well as moments when spiritual contact is not there. As inconvenient as that is for both myself and the client, I must be honest.

7. I will always focus my abilities for one's highest good and in a positive way. Everyone has free will. It is my intention to help one improve their energetic and spiritual life approach by allowing them to receive the information from me to help them move forward in life as they so choose.

Chapter 16

Why Go to a Psychic Medium?

I can tell you why I go to see a psychic medium. I find there are moments in my life when I feel I'm just not getting it clearly enough when information and signs are coming to me for me. Sometimes I find it hard to discern what is for me and how to take that information and direct myself. I look for ways to manifest what I need. If I feel there is some guidance available to me, I will go to a psychic medium to see if that guidance can be confirmed and acknowledged to me through someone who can connect with God and the Holy Spirit. Finding someone connected to God is not that hard. There are many fantastically guided and connected working psychic mediums who are offering services which are the same, or similar to what I have been offering. I find the information which I receive is profound, interpretable and important. I am not always impressed with the person I choose to receive a reading from and often try to find the purpose behind that as well. In addition, the medium part of a reading is healing. To be able to hear from someone the details and information which pertains to a loved one whom I have lost becomes a humbling experience to the connection I have. It is often that we may come across someone who unknowingly gives us information that allows us to skip the psychic medium all together. Anyone who crosses our path can give us divine information. I see this all the time.

Chapter 17

"Don't Read the Whole Me; Just What I Want You to Read and Some Future Prophecy Too!"

B locked information is impossible for me to read. If you are going to test me, then my intuition will be searching hard for that piece of information. If you are hiding that information, I will have a hard time finding anything for you. If you are hiding something that you don't want me to read into, then I won't. I do not work well with debunkers. I know they are there and they love to doubt and test me. I do look at it as a challenge at times, but my abilities are not for that purpose. A debunker is one who already decides I am wrong before we meet. A skeptic is different: they are more testing to prove to themselves. That is important; we should all be careful and be skeptic to a point.

Here is a story of one beautiful, skeptical woman who came to me. I was in my office channeling, while writing down information for this woman for about 10 minutes before she arrived at my office. I felt that she had relationship issues that she wanted to discuss, but was hiding her 'real feelings' about that relationship deep within her. I wrote that information down in short notes to relay to her once she arrived. In addition, I felt the presence of her father. Not sure if he was passed yet or not, I wrote down the words, "Dad finally comes with love." Now I was ready, trusted what information I had already received, and was excited for her to walk through the door so I could go deeper into the divine connections I already had prepared for her.

She came in, sat down in front of me and the first words out of her mouth to me were, "I am skeptical." I could not believe she did that. She unknowingly and instantly shut off all Divine and intuitive connections that I had for her. The only information I could give her was what I had written down and I had not the chance to share that with her before she told me of her skepticism. I sit with clients by the hour. I had to spend time within this session to relax and guide her to a place where she could feel comfortable. She had previously experienced a psychic reading with someone who was not ethical. I can understand how other experiences with other psychic mediums can be disappointing and have a lasting effect on someone, causing a deep skepticism. I simply told her, "You are here, you came, and we are doing this with or without your openness. You came with great faith and purpose lined with fear, but we are working with God, so let's go for it. If you are still uncomfortable, you can leave." I told her that I would have to earn her trust and that the energy I wanted to read, that was specifically for her, required her to release her free will a little bit so I could filter through God and through her energy. I wanted to give her the reading she deserved. I just handed her my paperwork of notes. I showed her the few lines of information I had received for her before she came. That softened her and allowed her to be more open, resulting in perfect healing communication with her father in spirit, as well as clarifying information about the relationship she was in. This session clearly needed to start out slow and delayed the connection which was ready before she was. So many times that happens when the clients are not prepared for their session. Reality is who can be 'prepared' for a session? No one is ever really ready to get the messages, but they come when they are ready. With compassion and expression of truth, the readings will be great.

If you do not feel it is the right time for you to be involved in a psychic reading, don't get involved. I want to make others feel comfortable. I feel no need to prove myself to anyone. If you do not believe, then that is your choice. Everyone feels how they do. When the time is right it will work out for you. Information is blocked to me when you feel that way. I will not invade your privacy. I have no right to impede on your free will. I often refer to it as this: If you are house-sitting, you "naturally" do not snoop and look through the person's personal spaces, such as drawers and closets. When I am with someone, I "naturally" do not snoop into their energy or aura. I do not have permission to invade your 'energy space' and unless I am working with you, I get to 'relax' and not have to receive. It is a natural ethical process.

I am not "on'" all the time, however I do not shut off either. How do you turn off your soul? When I am "on" and working for you, I would hope you will be open to me and not consciously hide things from me to "test" me. In no way am I going to judge you. It is not polite to ask a psychic medium, "What number am I thinking of?" It is almost degrading to the Divine meaning behind the spiritual connection for which you came. Although sometimes I can guess the number, it is just frustrating. The goal is to work with you and have you be comfortable and open. I must say that sometimes I can see through the walls someone might put up. If I can, that would be one of the reasons your soul directed you to me. Clients sometimes need to see and hear me comment on what they might be blocking. This is a healing for them. I am not going to see into that wall or through that skeptic energy unless it is divinely guided for me to do so. All which a psychic medium receives is with purpose.

CHAPTER 18

There Are Some Quick Rules and Guidelines to Consider Before Getting a Reading

* I do not read for anyone under the age of 18 without a parent or guardian's consent. This is done for the purpose of protection from the adolescent misunderstanding of what is being said simply due to the immaturity revolving around the age. A child needs to have guidance to bring later understanding to what might come through for them.
* You must wait six months to book another reading with me. Readings have information that can expand and travel timelessly. There is no reason to reconnect with a channel that is perfectly clear so soon. If you feel that need to see a psychic too often, then consideration of another resource to help bring focus may be needed, such as healing or therapy.
* I do not read or receive negative information pertaining to chronic illness or death. Unless you are already aware of a diagnosis, I do not receive that information. We all have the free will to learn and experience life without the invasion of the end of that life being present in our knowledge base. If you know that information, for yourself or others, there

is a forced 'idea' that this may happen and it is never the intention from God to allow you to feel that there is an end. Life is not a race, it is a ride.

* I do not read for skeptics. Skeptics choose to allow their free will to be read closed. The door is shut and without non-judgment, there will be no reading.
* I do not read you if you are drunk.
* The length of a reading can vary. Most readings use up an entire hour, but can be shorter. It depends on how much information you are looking for; how prepared with questions you may be; how much time spiritual communication takes, as well as what other combinations of psychic therapy are involved in your reading.
* Which rates to charge for this service become ethical and realistic choices to make. This ethical question comes with a vast amount of discernment. What I have to say about what I charge is, "Money is not my ruler". I often tell that if my life was parallel and I could choose how to work with this gift without having to adapt to the millennium, I would perch on a mountain. I would put myself out there to be reached, accepting food (chocolate) and company in return for the divine messages. This would make me happy, comfortable and allow me to reach all that wanted to come. Although this is not a reality for my path, I do feel there is a commitment to this gift that moves beyond the rate you charge. In addition, I do not see myself living a servant life on a mountain any time soon. Basically, if you are paying for something, you want to make sure you are receiving what you are paying for. What is offered depends on the fee.

Chapter 19

Come With Awareness of Your Own Ethics and Responsibility In Front Of You

I don't have to act professionally, but I do. You have responsibilities to consider when going for a reading of any kind. I am sharing my gift with you. I don't have to do it if I don't want to; it is my gift. During a session there are some things you need to do. Most important is to let the psychic medium know if they are right; make a connection; feel the channel as well; and make confirmation. It is a personal connection through me. My heart is always involved. My sensitivity and energy are involved and it is my most personal feelings and emotions which I allow the spirits to use to connect with me. I expect nothing but total respect for my human body from the spirits I communicate with.

Have respect for me as the intuitive. I am human. This is my gift I am sharing. I know my responsibility but I do have free will and a choice to not share. It is normal in society; we have a mindset which does not share naturally. While I am working, I am not in the selfish state; I am in a loving state. You have to have some respect for the work and take me seriously. In turn, I say this also so you do not just blow off an appointment. Nothing is more upsetting to a psychic medium than when you do not show up. I personally prepare for sessions before clients come by allowing information in. Don't just decide to not go and think, "Oh, she is a psychic. She probably already knows I'm not coming."

Have more respect for the intuitive who has taken on the responsibility to spiritually serve the community. It is hard to make appointments and have full intention of being open and to receive information for someone and then have them just not arrive. Sadly, I have to admit there have been times that I have channeled for clients who were 'no shows' and they did have loved ones who came to tell me they would connect if possible. Just the interaction which existed through making the session brings the information for that person. Remember there is no time associated to the messages received, so there could be information which comes from the intention of the session. If you miss a session appointment, call and make another one (if you are guided) or leave it alone if you feel you must.

Another point to consider is how many appointments you make for yourself. If you are going to have a reading, do not make another appointment with another psychic medium to have a reading done within days of the other. There needs to be some faith and consideration for the psychic medium with whom you are sitting. Respecting that person will bring a faith into what information is coming to you. It is important not to waste your money trying to prove something intuitively beyond you by comparing two psychic's readings. I know I enjoy hearing that I have confirmed and repeated something another intuitive might have said, but I am still concerned for the client who feels that instead of accepting and acknowledging the information, they are seeking to have more validation from an unverifiable source. Have faith that if you are guided and receive information, there is an amount of time you should wait to get another session. You can accept what you are receiving and if it is repetition, you have to accept there is a responsibility for you as the client to take on.

CHAPTER 20

Do The Messages From Heaven Always Come Through?

There are reasons I see the people I do. It is always beyond me how things work out. I will sometimes even become nervous before an appointment. It does not matter if it is one reading or a group session. I always know there is a possibility I might know nothing at all. I could be so wrong I would have to leave embarrassed. There is one time in particular I can recall. There was a woman who called for a mediumship session. This meant she wanted to have a reading consisting of just communication with the beyond. I had an office at the time and she drove about an hour to get to me. Once sitting with me, she folded her arms, sat back and just looked at me. She said nothing. I felt nothing. The moment was driving me to shake. I wondered what was happening. I pulled out my tarot cards to see if that would bring me any clarity. At that I said, "Ok, I feel a man with you. I feel this man could be a father figure and he is sending love." I wanted to be as specific as I could. I felt a man on her left side and very close. I felt no information coming as far as specific communication, so again I was at a standstill. Usually I do not ask the questions up front nor do I look for confirmation verbally, except that I was not reading her energy. She confirmed her father was in spirit. However she kept her arms folded and offered no other information. I finally told her, "I can't read you." I could not believe the words came out of my mouth. I had wonderful sessions before her that day and the day before. Never had I felt so abandoned. I knew there had to be a reason. "Well then read anything about me. Tell me all of the people around me that are dead. Tell me what I do for work or what I should be doing for work. Just tell me anything." With a deep breath I closed my eyes and felt I was on the sand and Jesus was holding me, as he took the footsteps for me. I felt comforted. Unfortunately, I had no information. I was blank. There was no time to analyze this. I told her I was sorry and embarrassed and not sure what to think.

At this time in my life I was just about to start venturing more into the public eye with my work. I was preparing classes and writing articles. I was enjoying the opportunities which I was being presented due to this gift and ability. Now what? "I'm sorry," I said, "I have not one piece of information coming to me. You owe me no money and I do hope that this experience will not in any way turn you away from going to see another psychic medium. I have to just accept this and hope that an understanding of 'why' comes." At that moment she started to talk and talk a lot; not too happy, but expressive. She said, "I was just told by a psychic medium last week that I am a psychic medium myself and that I m due to find my greatest spiritual guide here on Earth to help me with my mission. I have to also talk to spirits for my life mission."

She continued to say, "This other psychic medium told me that her name was 'Rebecca Anne' and I would find her on the Internet. I found you. I was looking for a mentor and it's obviously not you."

Little did she know that it was very obvious to me as well that I was not to be her mentor. How could I? She was testing my ability and my gift for the purpose of testing me. Am I the one? I do not work for anyone but God. I am not going to question why God chose for me to not become a mentor for this woman. He just did. I had to trust that intuition. Needless to say, all readings following her were complete with accuracy and channeled connections. I have never been abandoned by this gift. I may not always be as accurate as I strive for, but most of the time I am on target. If I am off target, I know it is just the matter in which I was receiving, or it is the manner in which the clients were rejecting what I was receiving. There may have been a higher purpose to why I did or did not receive what they were looking for. You have to have faith in the soul-connected information and its purposes. Either way, I trust all that God sends to me and I receive it openly.

CHAPTER 21

Psychic Mediums Can Be Wrong?

I am just a human being and with that there are always influences which can cause a low reading. How the psychic medium is feeling at the time of the reading (tired, sick, or maybe their mind is on something prominent in their lives) can affect the reading. At those times when I have clients, I will cancel. Not often, as I try to draw the strength from spirit to keep my commitments, but I will not keep an appointment with someone if I do not feel I can do my best through God for them. I may not always have that 100 percent accuracy I strive for, but that is directly due to the fact that I will not lie. I will not use my knowledge to mislead or persuade you into believing what I am saying. I will not purposely misinterpret. I will not make you feel uncomfortable at any time. Rather, I tell you all that I feel honestly and in every way. I do not worry that you do not understand. If you don't "get it" when we are together it may come to you in an hour, a day, or even months down the road. When I open up like that, even what I consider to be confusing and outlandish seems to always turn out making 100 percent sense to the person whom I am relaying my intuition to.

Here is a testimonial from a past client of prophetic information which did not connect at the time, but turned out to be profound for the client on many levels.

"My Reading with Rebecca: I had a wonderful phone reading with Rebecca, filled with many validations from the other side. In addition, she told me my brother was showing her a red "deflated" balloon in an office setting and she felt I would see this later as a sign of love. I told her I worked in a school but she insisted she saw the red deflated balloon at an office. She also told me to watch for balloons in general because she felt he would be showing them to me as a sign of his love. I confessed to Rebecca that it took a lot to convince the skeptical side of me that things like seeing butterflies, coins and hearing certain songs were actually signs.

"However, as soon as I came out of my room after the reading I came upon my teenage son who had been impatiently waiting for me to get off the phone. He was home sick that day from school, bored and had found a bag of gold balloons and was blowing them up and balloons were all over the house. I literally can't remember the last time we had balloons in our house (years) and I don't even know where the bag of balloons came from. About a week later, as I was walking out of my doctor's office I noticed a red "deflated" helium-type balloon in the parking lot. I got in my car and stared at it, wondering if it was a sign from my brother. Then the wind caught the balloon just right and moved it gracefully across the parking lot directly to my driver's car door where I could literally reach over and touch it. It said "I love you" on it. How perfect is that!"

CHAPTER 22

How a Psychic Reading Can Vary

When I sit with someone once, the reading may be fulfilling and open. I could answer a lot of questions. The second time I sit with that same person, their reading might be totally different. I may not answer a lot of questions, but I may have communication with a loved one for them who passed. If your life has not taken new turns and things are moving along slowly for you between readings, then your second reading may be full of information repeated from your last. What was important then may be the same important information now. Always think about, and ask questions about, how to plan or work your reading. If you would like to have the information come without questions, ask the psychic medium to give you a "general life reading", as they can always do that.

Every reading for every person is a little different. I find that no two readings run alike. I have seen and heard it all: from swinging couples, sex addicts, hypochondriacs, vocational candidates and true earthly saints to panic attacks, surprise planned parties, true gifts, past life energies, alien abductions, intuitive children and more. I have seen heartache and true soul mate loves. I have had guides give me all the information for someone's reading. I never know what I am going to come across until I get there. What happens from there is what is meant to be when my energy interacts with someone. I have tuned into that ability so I can have a humbling understanding of how each soul is unique and each person's path is individual to them.

CHAPTER 23

Where Are The Dead People
That Mediums Talk To?

Who knows? God knows? The dead people, do they know where their soul is living? They are in a place of consciousness which is full of love and pure information. They love us and miss us so they make sure to be around us. We are all part of the same universal energy which connects us to this place where they are. I call this place Heaven. Until we die, we will not know for sure what happens. I believe we leave the concreteness of the earth when we leave our body. We shed our outer energy, as it is no longer needed. The soul retains all memory and becomes all-knowing. This idea of coming out of the darkness of the human body and entering the brightness of knowing God brings justification to the Christian idea of beatific vision. The souls with whom I have spoken are without a physical form. I believe we reincarnate if we so choose. I also believe we will most likely choose to return to another physical existence to have miraculous experiences once again in human form. There are a large number of unknown and improvable pieces of information about the afterlife. What I know for sure is that they are somewhere at peace with other souls, happy, loving, healthy and always wanting the best for their loved ones.

CHAPTER 24

Healing Purpose to Connecting
to the Spiritual Realm

There are four top things which the dead tell me. 1) We are happy. 2) We are healthy. 3) We are full of love. 4) Why aren't you talking too …? Yes, when you have a family member here who you are not speaking to that is connected to the loved one in spirit, you can bet your bottom dollar they will call it out. It is very important to them that we recognize how important our soul family is, whether it is biological or not.

It is important to have a realization of our loved ones being beyond. Once this happens, then we have to understand how connecting with our loved ones can heal. It is not just healing; it is a way to prepare for what is to come in one's own life. Think of how grief is an extension of what you think is going to happen to you, as well as what has happened to the one who has just passed. There is this realization that you really don't know, and yet we do. Most have grown up with the idea of Heaven or Hell. Believe me, everyone gets into Heaven. We will have our faith restored when we think about and connect with our loved one's souls who greet us as we cross. We will have peace and you will have calmness knowing they are fine, they are there, and they are with us as well.

Connection to the dead allows us to realize there is no such thing as death, but life in a new form through a rebirth to pure soul. Connecting to ones who have passed on is exactly that: they have passed on into another dimension but they have not died, not in the way we view death as an ending, but as a beginning. If you have ever studied the tarot deck of cards, the death card does not mean someone is going to die, but it means that one's energy has shifted in order for a new path to emerge. The healing of a "beyond" connection is the "knowing" that spiritual death does not exist. I think it is also very healing to realize that no matter what you do in this lifetime and no matter whom you are or where you have been, you will be transformed; you will experience this rebirth and you can not fail. That is how faith works and that is the message of the dead. They are a lighter energy accepting love and trying to share it with you.

The other magical energetic side to connections is the feeling of calmness; that we are one and we are a part of each other. Being around a soul with such light energy and high vibration allows you to experience what it feels like to be free from your mind while reveling in your spirit. When connecting with a loved one or guide from Heaven, I know you will also react to the physical and emotional feelings being presented as the medium is within this experience. There is energy which is expansive and available for all to feel. Learning to recognize on your own the feeling you receive when you know a loved one is around can bring much enlightenment into your life as it awakens your intuition.

I have to say I take the responsibility to communicate with loved ones who have crossed with grave seriousness. It is a deeply profound experience to have a psychic medium, who is also just a normal human being, connecting to someone who has left their loved ones behind. It is a physical connection to the energy being sent from Heaven and attaching itself to our human bodies. There is a lot of responsibility to acknowledge when it comes to sharing that information. Every medium you approach should retain that same ethical mindset. If you have an experience which is within your own mediumship, consider the power in that encounter and acknowledge it. It is a manifestation of your soul's intuitive connections.

CHAPTER 25

Why Should Someone Not Go For A Reading?

First, let's start with some true signs that it is a gifted psychic medium. When the information you receive feels settling to your heart and comfortable to your energy, that right there is a sign of a gifted psychic medium. There are a few realistic signs which you can see as well. It is awesome and meaningful when accurate signs come through without any prompting questions. It is common for a good psychic medium to receive names, dates and status of situations. There is a sense of complete understanding and flow from a gifted intuitive which has purpose and meaning, alongside those tidbits of information that make perfect sense.

If you have been going to intuitive after intuitive with the same questions or topics, and receiving the same information but not learning or growing from it, you may have to consider what you are or are not doing to cause that common outcome. Is there some information you did not act on? You have to consider that you should not go for a reading if you are feeling or noticing you are depending on them. A good psychic medium, with an awareness of spiritual ethics, should tell you if you are stuck, rebelling or ignoring the meaning of the information they are receiving for you. If you need to know your next move all the time and there is a psychic willing to take your money to tell you that next step, you should not go to them for a reading, as they are enabling you. You do not need to know the next step, as that will happen no matter what and you should not pay someone to live your life for you.

You should also not go to a psychic medium if you are searching for an answer which is not for your highest good.

A true psychic medium should not offer you spells, curses or incantations to bring enlightenment through to you. If you feel you really have a physical reason why you are having issues which might need to be directed to a doctor first, then do so. If you are unstable, a psychic reading may not be able to balance you. You have to take care of yourself. If you are guided still, then go. Intuitive information alongside traditional treatment may bring the clarity you need. They work quite well in conjunction, but not in excess.

There are warning signs you should avoid. Again, follow your heart and know that when you get that duck and dodge feeling, call and cancel. You do not have to give reasoning. It is the reason itself that you felt that way and followed through. That is instantly a way for you to follow your own intuition. You have to take caution to protect your energy when you go with an intention to be open for someone to accurately connect for you. Be aware of questions. Too many can lead a talented, but deceptive, person. Many claim they are intuitive, but read your face and body language as a profession, bringing a lot of analyzing on their behalf following specific questions they pose to you, as well as how they ask them. There are the downright dark and evil, mean-looking psychic mediums who may be perfect for you, however you may want to consider where their information is coming from, as well as the ramifications of what that information may hold for you. You are good with God. Others may be informative and accurate but accomplish their goal through negativity. I have received great mini-readings from booths at fairs; profound channeling from beachside boardwalks; and spiritual connections from local expos. It is where you are guided which brings you that guidance.

CHAPTER 26

How Do You Know Which Psychic To Go To?

I s it a matter of faith and direction versus selfish need? I believe that each intuitive has a unique gift; research into who and where you go to get guidance is very important. There are some who I am guided to that others are not. Some are guided to me and I feel that is because God felt I was the one to receive for that person. You can go to one psychic and love it, have your best friend go to the same psychic and be disappointed. Each of us receives what we are supposed to from the people we are going to connect with. There is a great sense of faith necessary when picking a psychic which needs to be acknowledged.

Why should you go to a psychic medium at all? The connection itself which a psychic medium has to the channel God provides for us does one important thing. It brings us closer to God. It connects our living soul with the beyond to which it longs to be connected. We have a soul which loves to receive information from the home from where it came. We go to learn the reason why we are here and confirmation of our own intuitive, knowing that at times, we all have a hard time seeing clearly. One may choose to go to clear away confusion, frustration or grief; another may go for a different perspective on current situations. Others feel it is fun or entertainment and embrace the experience as a moment to connect with possibilities beyond their awareness. All of these reasons and more are perfectly in alignment with the job a psychic medium is ready to do for you.

How Should Someone Prepare For A Session With A Psychic Medium?

B efore a session: When the decision is made to embrace this connection through a psychic medium, it is important to remember that although they do not have the control to give you all that you want, there is a sense of trust needed. You need to trust that what comes through for you will be the result of God's blessing on you to receive what is for your highest good. With that said, you can prepare for this encounter by opening up your energy and focusing that energy around you, so that you may be read more accurately. If you are open, the connection is easier. One way which I suggest to be in alignment for a reading is to take a moment to write down your intentions for the session. Put it down on paper. There are some great ways to help bring more guidance from the human being receiving for you. Having those human traits, like the ego and self interpretations which are unique to us all, we all interpret differently. Here is an example of how you can prepare a sheet of questions or topics. This also includes the mention of loved ones in spirit.

For my highest good I would like to know about:

- My relationship with my husband and how to heal it
- My relationship with my daughter and how to enhance it
- Ways to advance my financial issues through resolutions at work
- My health and the emotional attachments which I can release to improve the harmony of my being with love and from love

For my highest good I would like to hear from:

- My grandmother -- what advice does she have? What messages can she share to connect me to her love?
- My Brother -- whom I miss. I welcome messages from him.

It does not have to be more than that. Simple and understandable puts a clear line of purpose out there with a positive intention. There do not have to be details. Some people will bring a physical item with them to connect to the loved one they want to talk to. This is okay, but I prefer to not know about it at all! Put it in your pocket and keep that energy and love close. I will pick up the item more often if it is not presented as a guessing game. It is more profound when people have that item and I just mention it out of the blue, as the loved one usually tells me about it. This allows me to receive without the ego in the way. The intentions you write down should also stay in your pocket, as they are also a production of energy. I do not need to see them or even confirm that you have them. Toward the end of the session it is always good to pull it out and reference if there was anything missed that you might have the opportunity to still ask about.

During a session: Stay aware, open, and take notes. It is important that, beyond the spiritual responsibility to accept what is coming, you have to be in a state of awareness to acknowledge what you are receiving. Take notes or bring a recorder to allow yourself to have this channeling available for future reference. It is so important to understand that what you receive at that moment may not come to settle within you as accurate and confirming until hours, days, weeks or years after the session; once life takes on that specific course. You are to interpret your session. The fact is these sessions and experiences were filled with information from God to you. Great gifts for your soul are being shared. This psychic medium is working for and connecting in the right way to bring you this information. So to take the notes is very important.

If I go to see a psychic medium, I have to be very open. I understand there are hard people to read as I come across it enough to recognize the mental process. I am willing to admit I am a skeptic of my own profession. Even after taking notes, I may still be closed off. It can take me quite a while to accept what has been said. I have to go back and reread the notes of the session quite a few times. There are few psychic mediums which I have had sessions with that I trust. Deb, a truly gifted psychic medium and healer, is the first I trusted which filled me with the realization that there are many of us working as psychic mediums that are "real". She was accurate, loving, and read for me with compassion and willingness. She is more to me a guide in this lifetime than she may ever realize. I can feel and trust within my heart to open to her. Everyone has an opportunity to meet an intuitive like Deb; someone to receive messages from, someone to gain clarity through, and someone to help confirm for you what you are already manifesting into your life.

You have to put aside your judgments and just decide to be open now so you can look back objectively. This is "easier said than done". If you have experienced psychic mediums having a hard time reading you, then consider that you may have to put more trust in the fact that this human being in front of you, indeed may have a gift for you for your highest good. Trust that you are being guided for a reason. Have reasoning behind why you are going which will affect your overall purpose in life.

Confirmation is also important to the reader during a session of any kind. You have to make sure that you give confirmation. If you receive a piece of information and the reader starts to repeat it, analyze it, etc. You have the responsibility to share with them what you can confirm and what you can not. This should only be done with non-descriptive answers limited barely above a "Yes" or "No". The reason for this is simple.

We want to have the opportunity to share with you the entire impression and not have you share with us something we may have received. Imagine the door we are opening, just the first in a series which will bring us deep within the connection to information. Each piece of confirmation, just from a simple "Yes" can open the next door for us to move into the next piece of information. It is an active process which you are involved in mentally, physically, energetically, and spiritually. It is to be enjoyed!

During a session be open on another level as well. Do not be surprised to feel and accept the same information which is being channeled for you by the psychic medium. It is possible; it can happen and the result can be double confirmation for all involved. As we each receive uniquely, the information can bring double meanings as well as double intensity filled with information and verification. Be open to feel the love from a soul in Heaven. Bring yourself to envision a path which is set before you and see where that leads. Feel, if you agree with the channel, and ask questions if you need to.

After a session: Revel in the fact that your soul just connected God! The mission of the experience was to bring you closer to God through a soul connection to intuitive information from beyond. It was an experience which our souls are divinely and actively aware of. They leap for joy within our human body as the slightest connection.

Your notes are yours; the experience should be thought about and considered. If it was not a good reading, there is an opportunity to think about why. Was the reading or the psychic medium "bad"? Each experience has its own individual outcome, just as each of the readings is unique to the psychic medium. If you felt the information was accurate and the guidance was realistic, act upon it. You came for a reason, got the answer and have a light on that path. If it is truly for your highest good and it was the answer to your seeking, then take that responsibility to proceed. Take that next step to embrace what God has planned next for you. If you need to heal, forgive, retreat or embrace someone or something as it was a topic channeled for you, and it is accurate and was needed information, take it to heart. Do with it what you want to, as you have free will.

CHAPTER 28

"Do You Think That When People Seek Counsel From Psychics That it Affects Their Energy or the Energy of the Situation, Either in a Good Way or a Bad Way?"

An interesting question I received one day also brings awareness to what your energy can experience from a psychic medium. It is in quotes below. The question was an email reading which I answered within the question, as I do when I channel for all readings through the Internet. "Do You Think That When People Seek Counsel From Psychics That It Affects Their Energy..." YES!!

"or the energy of the situation..." Not the energy of the situation itself, but the energy coming from the person receiving confirmation or enlightenment on that particular situation. If their energy changes, their view changes and the energy that they "give" toward the situation changes, then there is an effect on the situation. It is energy cause and effect.

". . . either in a good or a bad way?" This part for me is important. You will never have a bad result from a session with me of any kind. I am connected to God, have faith and trust. That is how I receive. If you are at a psychic for guidance and this psychic is crap, a liar, not connected to God, etc., you take the chance that the information he/she gives you; changing your "thoughts" (therefore changing the "energy" you "send out") could have a bad effect. That is just the truth! You are going to a psychic to bring an understanding and awareness to your inner soul's desires. This is done through manifestation. It is important to understand and acknowledge what manifestation is. In a way, the manifestation of our soul's desire is very important. It is our focus on the driver's seat as we embrace the back seat driver role. There is the constant desire to take over and gain understanding. We can all relate to this on some level. I can. Even if a psychic medium is just a stepping stone toward enlightenment, I feel there is a need to embrace and hug your psychic as a part of your path.

CHAPTER 29

Needing to Have Life Experiences Without Intuitive Help

There are other reasons why, other than my own inability to read someone, information may not come. This ability has the limitation of free will. We all have free will and I will not receive for someone if it is not meant to be for them to know right now for their highest good. The timing may be wrong for the person. The connection or information may not come to me in any other way than to say nothing. I believe someone can be at a point in their lives when they must do things on their own. They can ask for help and seek out New Age advice, but it may not be there for them yet. The key word is "yet". I have had light readings for someone at their first reading, but connect everywhere with them the second and third time I sit with them. I do not do readings for someone more than one time in a six-month period. I feel if you need to come to me more than once in six months, I may not be what you need. There might be an issue for a spiritual director or therapist. Time needs to pass before I speak intuitively with them again. When doing case work, that is different. I will read and reread whatever I need to, seeking more information trying to make a case move forward. A client's life is moving forward without me. God has plans for all of us. If it is part of the plan for me to be there, then I am. In turn, we all have to take responsibility for the actions we take after we receive intuitive information from any resource.

Writing things down when I speak helps me to focus. I don't always do this, but if I can draw what I see, the visual can make more sense than the way I verbalize the thought. This is a form of automatic writing. There are smells of all sorts which can come through. I often use clairscent and associate smoke smells or food smells with someone in spirit. There could be a new car smell when associated to purchasing a new car or fresh paint with remodeling. It is not that the person actually carries the smell on them physically, but more of a sensing the smell in my mind's eye and reading that information through my sense of smell as I read their energy.

Sometimes I hear, through clairaudience, the music, singing, trains, bells or whatever my mind's eye is sensing from that energy I am focusing on which can be interpreted through my sense of hearing. If I have a sensation, then I explore it. I don't drive myself crazy. When I hit a roadblock and if what I have said about a thought I received seems dead-ended, I'll move on. If I think about something too long it becomes more confusing. I have to try to fight my ego and my rational mind from interrupting. That never helps the sessions along. Trust that what I say may not make sense at first but, in time, all intuitions work themselves out. If I push too hard on one thought while seeking confirmation, I could start to "consciously" rationalize what I am saying. That is not the purpose behind receiving information from beyond. It is not from within you, it is from the "outside in".

CHAPTER 30

An Attunement Just For You!

"At this time I would like to attune you. I would like you to visualize with me. Take this moment to think that above you there is a spiral of beautiful energy -- any color that feels good to you. Feel this energy swirling about and being present as energy. Now feel that there is a funnel cloud or beam of light that comes down from this present cloud-like energy above you. It is always there, always has been there and always will be there for you. You have a crown chakra above your head; you can open the top of your head and allow that energy from above to attach to your spirit, your body, your mind and your energy. All that energy is flowing through your human being. It is a peaceful and pleasant energy that allows you to receive all that wants you to connect with. You have always had this connection and can bring that energy into yourself. At any moment, you can consider yourself connected! Your soul was always connected to that energy. Remember that energy is from where your soul comes. At this point, you have been attuned to acknowledge that connection is there. Enjoy. Blessings to You."

CHAPTER 31

Who Cares What Your Foundation of Belief Is?

C atholicism is the background and root of my beliefs
and gifts. My abilities were given to me directly from
God through the Holy Spirit. Catholics are not the only
organized, or not organized, religion which acknowledges
there is a soul and a God. I am aware of the fact there are
many different names and references to and about God. The
Higher Power, Mother Earth, and Spirit Guides; they all fit
into my readings. All of this can fit into any reading with
any psychic medium connected to God, as that brings in
the accurate and purposeful information pertaining to your
specific path location at the time of that reading.

I am a woman of the millennium and I am aware of
11:11, UFO's, ghosts, portholes, and conspiracies, Indigo
Children, Planet X and more. I am open-minded and will
not judge. How can I? He who casts the first stone? Not
me. I find that my God can have a simple analogy to an
umbrella which covers me. If God is my center, my top
point, my balancer when placed down, all that comes down
under that umbrella of protection for me is from God. He
will only allow in what is supposed to be. I will accept with

faith and trust that which feels right. What is from God, whether it falls within my religion or not, is important to me as I understand there is much outside that small box which is not to be missed.

For me it is always important to channel, to connect, and to be aware of what is needed. Having been raised with a strong religious foundation, I find that I can honor what I have always felt. I have embraced my religious past as an acknowledgment of where I am supposed to me. It is the religious rituals and history which is the inner part that I feel is within my being. I am educated in other religions, yet my soul desire has always been to accept what I have been given as a foundation.

If there was a reason to lie, would you? White lies? When I am working I do not have the capacity to use a lie. I could lie; I have the ability and I know many false psychics who do lie. Again, there is a trust that one should have. I have this trust to accept what is coming. I do not receive what is not for our soul advancement, so if it comes to me during a session, you get it all. It all has purpose and what I see is not for me to lie about. I have to have faith, even if it does not make sense. Again, I have to have faith. We all have to have that faith in our lives, to accept what is coming, to figure out why. It usually does not benefit you if you lie to yourself. I have to put full trust in the gift that I have. Once I have received an impression on a topic for you, I will tell you what it is. If you do not agree or you do not understand what I am telling you, I will not change my statement to accommodate your views. Often it takes time (days, weeks, or months) for someone to understand the full meaning of some of the information I receive for them. In order for me to have the true impressions I want for you to come through, I have to be objective. I have to leave that ever-present ego out of the meaning of the message I comprehend for you.

CHAPTER 32

Is a Psychic Medium a Prophet?

We are all prophets of the millennium. Did you know that the role of a prophet is to look to the future to explain the present, not to look to predict the actual future?

The Bible is clear to point out that prophets did exist and their roles and abilities changed to adapt to the society and time in which they lived. I feel the prophets living in this millennium are actively sharing this duty and mission to adapt to our current social environment. A prophetic person is seen to have a psychic gift to see the future by powers of divination. That word "divination" means to attempt to discover the unknown through oracles, omens and mystical powers. It is receiving a feeling about something to come. That rings true to me now in this millennium in which we live. As a psychic medium, are we not also here to receive and give information to each other? I must adapt to society in such a way that I can be openly reached. If people are to be guided to me, I need to be out there expressing what it is I do in a truthful way. This is why I can condone someone now, in the modern millennium, referencing themselves as a prophet. How wonderful it is to receive divine information.

"Nabi" is the origin of the word "prophet" in English, meaning "one who speaks on behalf of another", as well as in Hebrew where it means "one called or one who is called". This prophet is a messenger of the divine decisions from Heaven to earth. This is said to happen, once having been in the presence of God and his angels, with the intentions to speak to others what God has already spoken. If it has already been spoken, as a prophet we have no timeline or issue with picking it up and sharing it. It is receivable information.

One of the most interesting, unifying themes seen throughout the Old Testament is the idea of prophets. It is seen as a reference in each book, if examined closely enough. There is a mention of receiving God's information through story and timeline, as well as in everything that has been done. I find it surprising how the prophets themselves are not reared as heroes in more of a conscious way through religious practices.

The fear is there still, for many parts of religions, to accept the title "psychic medium". However, in the modern world there are many limitations on what to call yourself if you are one. If I wanted to, I could say I am a prophetess. That would describe what I do; how connected to God I am; verification through accuracy; divine inspiration and spiritual fulfillers with spreading the messages. A prophet. Could you imagine how bold you have to be to call yourself a prophet in today's society, without having a stigma put on you that you are a bit crazy? Well for all of you out there, who call yourself a prophet or feel that you are, I am right with you! I feel I do fit that standing definition of a prophet. I do feel I am a prophet. I love that it is possible to connect yourself in that way. Who is going to tell you that you can't call yourself what you truly feel inside. If you feel connected, then you are. Are we not all prophets?

I often explain that some of the information I am receiving is 'prophetic' in nature, meaning I am receiving a piece of information which is important and meaningful for your personal future. I connect with the times of the great Biblical prophets and believe the nature of my work formed its foundation from that past.

I do believe as long as you are aligned in the right place, for the good of humanity and with perfect harmony within your soul-connection to your intentions, the information will be accurate, important and it will fulfill purpose. Will it be an experience directly connected to God as the stories are told in the Bible? Maybe, but I believe those times have been gone for a while. There is the opportunity, but I do not believe that humanity, as a whole, would accept that. Moses was the last to see God face-to-face. That was an intense time for prophetic information. Nor has anyone had such powers, such as parting seas, in a long time. However, I do see miracles daily within healings and intuitive sessions which have had the same profound effect on a human's soul as the blind faith of humanity in the Biblical times of ancient prophets.

Some prophets in the Old Testament tried really hard not to be prophets. They tried not to do what God wanted them to do, and it did not work. It is hard to become who you really are meant to be when the world around you is not always supportive. There is a higher purpose for which we are here. We have all heard that before, but how many of us really believe it? We are all here for purpose. We all have this ability and, to some point, I believe we should all be connecting and open to what our path is here on earth; a responsibility to listen to our souls to be happy and have love. A prophetic message is accurate and meaningful to the time period and the issues which society is going through at that time. I know that present day psychic mediums have the ability to channel through what is important to what will relate to today's issues.

People did listen to the prophets of the past and society learned and advanced on a collective soul level as a result. Now, in today's society, is it really that hard to comprehend the possibility that modern "normal" people could actually receive messages from that same source and have profound meaning for the people who hear these messages? I feel this is possible and happens all the time. We can choose to believe a scientist telling us of an upcoming ecological disaster, or we can ignore him. The burden is on the scientist who has to tell us the facts and then make us believe it. His gift is to share this; his path is to express this need to humanity. We are all aware of this need to repair the earth and redirect our relationship to where we live and breathe. His gift of knowledge is not readily received by all. He could be "debunked", blacklisted, ignored and more.

We don't want to move away from the norm in which we are living, but the channeled information is there, with or without scientific information to back it up. We know this just by opening our hearts and minds and looking around. But the scientist is someone with whom we can debate and fight. A psychic medium is one who is receiving information to help others as well, and in many ways, to help people save themselves. That information, too, must be taken seriously.

Indeed, I am coming from a place of love and peace. We are all blessed with that spirit! We all are moving, vibrating and connecting. It is the acknowledgement and awareness of the connection which is awakened through intuitive connection. I believe we are currently living within that New Age once again and that those concepts are again within our reach. We can all see and feel that the world has been moving in a new direction. This is scary, but it is a rebuilding of our humanity on all levels. It is wonderful to think of the future as bright for our children's children versus a gloomy forecast on what can not be changed. Do we not yet see this propheticness being shared by people who want to rebuild the economy and bring more focus to the destruction of the earth and the environments within which we live? God shares his messages with us clearly; it is up to us to listen. When we hear Him, we have to accept that we are all prophets.

CHAPTER 33

Your Gift of Knowing, Healing and Connecting to Intuition

A story about naturally-aware children and ducks . . .
I often notice how little children seem to be so connected and open to the energy within which I work. They seem to communicate so clearly with spirits and they have a knowing that is so pure and honest. I do not believe this is because they are naive. Is it possible for these children to have the future in their hands? To have that option is profound. How could that happen to someone? How can children be born with an ability to have intuition at their fingertips? Then I realized that they do and that they are connected quite clearly and innocently. Are ducks not born to swim? I wonder, if you never expose a duck to water, what would happen if throughout their life. What would they be like if they were never exposed to water? Would they then have to be reminded they can indeed swim? Like us, we are all children whom God has blessed with a soul and to the connection that exists beyond that. We are His children. We may not have retained or accepted that we have this connection, but once exposed

to it again; when it is the "right time" for us to be exposed to it, the ability will be available to us to be awakened and use it as it was naturally supposed to be. We all should expose ourselves to experiences which help awaken our inner path.

Our society is quick to either put down, or dispose of and ignore, any reference to the beyond and the unexplainable and paranormal. In many ways it is feared or ignored. It is more "entertainment" to society worldwide than something 'spiritual.' Fortunetellers at fairs were, and still are, a spectacle of enlightenment and enchantment which tries to entice you and draw you in. At one time I was hired to work as a psychic under a casaba tent, alongside belly dancers and henna artists at an outdoor entertainment venue where bands came to play. I was doing 45 readings per hour. People would stand in line and I would just give them what I felt from one spread of the tarot cards, then hand them one of my business cards and move to the next. After a while I noticed that people were getting back in line to receive more information instead of watching the concert they came to see. It was fun and meaningful to me even though I was not in my element.

Children love this kind of interaction; something not believed to be real, something fun. Children or teens are seen to dive into things like the Ouija boards without a second thought. They have a curiosity toward that beyond and unknown due to the natural rebellion which one feels toward authority telling them "No". Some parents raise their children and do not mention to them or confirm for them that the souls of our loved ones are around us all the time; that we are just here for a lifetime within this body, but our souls will live on. When these souls start to appear to the little children, parents are quick to say that it is their imaginations. That is not a good idea. It is clearly taking the water away from the duck!

One story I can tell is of my son who, at two years old, was singing with a spirit at the bottom of my stairs. I was getting ready to go to work and felt a spirit around as I often do before going to meet with the clients. Instead, my son was connecting to this spirit. I finally asked him who it was. He answered with a shrug of his shoulders and I could see him fall out of contact with that spirit at that second. It was as if his conscious mind became aware of the fact that he was interacting with a spirit which was not physically present. I just asked him what she looked like. He said, "She had on an orange shirt and black pants." I was excited to hear him respond and I told him that she must have been a great singer because he seemed to enjoy her. He responded with a small smile and walked away. That evening, my clients were connecting with their loved one who was buried dressed in black pants and a peach shirt. I did share with them the story of what my son did and said. How could I not?

This same child, now at the age of four, interacted again with a soul while coloring Valentine hearts. He had laid out three hearts with colors to match. All of my children were sitting at the table. My oldest and I looked at each other with shock as my son started to have a conversation about coloring his hearts with "someone" to his right, as I was on his left. No one was there that I was connecting with. It was for him, so I said, "Who are you talking to?" He answered with, "That man right there." I said, "Is he talking about your hearts?" "Yes," he said, "if I don't color them he said that he will, but he is just kidding." I was mouth wide-open, not sure who it was and not sure what to say. My oldest and I just looked at each other again with amazement; what happened next was profound to me as well. My oldest daughter (14 at the time) stood up and said, "Go ahead Mom and tell him what it is all about; that is your special thing." It was as if I was given permission to share the knowledge of Heaven to my son from my daughter who agrees and knows herself, as she also has her own connections.

The guidance that I needed to interact with my children comes from my children. To let you know how important it is to guide your children's openness and spirituality is profound. It is also easy, just follow their lead and keep the truth in front of them so there is no fear for them.

My point is to let you know how important it is to share with your children that it is not scary; and to reinforce that they can indeed interact with souls. Let them know they have a soul. That will be very comforting to them to know they are something special that never dies. These interactions come through a blessed connection to spirit through their souls. It is a divine gift from the Spirit which they are born with. On whatever level you look at it, you can not just tell the child different kinds of religious and esoteric information. I did tell my son as much information as I felt his four-year-old mind could handle. I discerned, as his parent and nurturer, what I felt he needed to know about these experiences.

I asked my son about that event with the man and asked if he knew who it was; he told me "nope". I then stopped asking him questions, as I knew the realization was coming to him that the man was not in physical form. So I told him that. "This man was not in a body, only his spirit was here. That is like a "see-through man"; a superhero with a lot of love who can use that 'love power' to talk to you; just you. And you can share that information with me and your family anytime someone comes. If you know a spirit is here, they come because they love you and someday you will see them again in Heaven."

In a way, the reality for a child is to know that someday the body will die. It is true. I also felt that my son at four is too young to grasp the idea of death and so I did not mention that; although he has told me, on many occasions, "he knows that before we were babies, we were alive". He knows that there is a place he can talk to that is beyond the world he lives in. He just knows it, as I feel, just as a duck can swim; children are attached to where they came from as an existence. Nurture that in the way you feel you can for your children and all the children you will ever come across and interact with. That is a lesson and blessing to be able to connect with each other. Love!

CHAPTER 34

Using Your Free Will to Accept From Messages from Heaven Outside of a Religion

There is a fear which penetrates the religious organizations worldwide when this topic of intuition is brought up to those not in full understanding of how powerful this connection can be. I am a Roman Catholic, born and raised. I have not left my faith. I can say I am "mostly" faithful at attending Mass and participating in the community aspect of the church to which I belong. I am a Catholic; I believe in the faith of that church with my whole being. In addition to that, I believe in so much more. I use this foundation of moralistic, ethical and spiritually-connected religion as a basis for my life and my reason for working as a psychic medium. Like I said, if it wasn't for Jesus, how would I be able to speak to our loved ones? He opened the gates of Heaven for us all. All of us! All souls! No matter what religion you are, He did that for all of our humanity.

To do the work I do, knowing I am connected, I take great acceptance this was a gift for me to use and share. I understand my path when it comes to the responsibility I have when sharing and working with these gifts. I am not afraid. With the faith and trust I have, I know these talents and abilities are within me and connected to me for a reason. How could it not be a gift? Information comes not just when I hope to have it come, like when I am with a client, but it also comes when I least expect it. To be able to know I am receiving this information and that I am able to share it usually has a profound change on someone's life.

CHAPTER 35

Angels and Guides

The reality for me is the connections I make with those in spirit are not the "angelic" messages which come through. I think about the two angels in the Bible, Michael and Gabriel. A psychic medium connected to Spirit can accept any information for a client from whichever source it is coming. When receiving directly from the highest of the high, information is divine and you can trust that they can discern for you. That information is for your highest good. I have had many beautiful healing and learning experiences involving information I receive from angelic beings. One client I remember very well had lost a close family member. I felt he was still so close by and often stayed in the home next to her for days on end. She loved this, but the energy was draining her. She believed in angels and felt they were messengers for her. I felt a vibration come into the room, one slightly like the essence of a human soul, however there was no one direction of information and instead it was all encompassing. I felt that angel instantly within my heart. The messages from that angel to her about her loved one were profound, healing, and full of enlightenment about her specific connection to this loved one. I will always remember the clear vibrational feelings from that angel.

Biblically, there is endless information about angels; they are mentioned in the Old and New Testaments over 200 times. One thing to mention about angelic information is that it often comes with direct commands and information to help. They are known to reveal important messages. They also guide you, protect you, and deliver your prayers to Heaven; they provide for you. The most beautiful job an angel can do for us is to bring us to Heaven when we cross over.

Accurate and inspirational communication is unique in its intention for one's spiritual growth in life. The guides are vast and varied. They could be loved ones we lost who are now our guides or guardian angels. They are also important Christian souls from the past such as saints and prophets; they are gods from Egyptian and Middle Eastern lands. They are often mythical by definition, or even animals with human animation. I have even had some situations where the guide was just indescribable. Regardless of whom they are, I accept the information from them for my clients as it is important for them on their life path. I have the greatest guides myself who are of the hierarchy in the realm of Heaven. To accept that connection was a profound gift which I now share with my clients as well. You can find people who are masters within their modalities which can connect you with the guides to which you are most attached. A medium who channels just your loved ones in spirit is focused information and you should share that, if it is your intention. The information about your angels can come from someone who is learned in a modality that focuses on angelic information only. There are animal communicators who will connect with and communicate with animals which are here or in spirit. There are so many New Age and spiritual or metaphysical practitioners out there, the access to these resources is endless.

CHAPTER 36

"Oneness" Discovered Through Self-Skepticism

I know we are all here with capable souls to connect with the beyond. We all have a bit of skepticism attached to the fear of the unknown. When I channel and receive information it comes to me, through me, and within me. I am aware of it at all times and take the responsibility to share it verbally or with automatic writing. Some messages can come with insistence through the Holy Spirit, resulting in written articles or information to be shared. This book is part of that very process. It has been Divinely given through me with great understanding and determination.

One night I was coming home from visiting the neighbors and was excited to finish up an article I was writing on manifestation. The neighbors and I had been debating the idea of "collective" energy, or entities within "oneness" of information channeling, instead of how I usually receive it with one through me, just one. I had just finished listening to a new tape which was "channeled information" from a resource which was collective, but took on one name. I have met many people who channel this way. I have even had students in my mediumship classes who have channeled the most beautiful information from whom they described as "they" or "us". I had not done that at all. I felt that the "we" they always spoke with was not right. I did not do it, so why did other mediums? My opinion was that the oneness was more general than, and not as individualized as, my channeled information. I acknowledged that it was another technique to channel for readings as well, with the "we" giving the intuitive information.

Now back to the night coming home from the neighbors: Strangely, as I walked up my own driveway, in my head I heard "we will help you write your article, but first you must let us tell you about the oneness so you can accept your channel of 'we' when you need it." Now I was not too quick to put this off, but my wall of skepticism rose in my stomach. I became nervous and aware of my judgments up to this point. With a deep breath, I said out loud "No, not without Christ." I was testing this energy which was connecting to me. Back I received, "Okay when you are ready, with Christ, we will help you." I was shocked and overwhelmed with a feeling of peace. So I went inside, sat at the computer and the following is exactly what I channeled. I put it in quotes because I feel the information was not from me, but completely and clearly, cleanly and purposefully through me.

"Understanding Oneness: What is Heaven? Where are the souls of those who have passed? There is a way to understand oneness; knowing there are some common answers which are understandable, will let you know how God is so powerful. The uniqueness of us all is the soul. When the soul is referenced, there is individuality, the wholeness of one and there is the reality of oneness among us all, making us all one and connected for all reasons purposeful. Within this "oneness" we can seek out the plans and purposes of life within our own souls. Make connections and get answers. Finding satisfaction at all costs as this oneness is God's love. It is not a "concept" that we become "one". The purpose for living in our human bodies would not exist. There would be nothing to learn, gain, or advance. It is for our souls to share information with that oneness as a resource for us and for you.

"Consider how powerful God's love is and how full of information this "collective" spirit is the Holy Spirit. We will all help. We, as a collective energy, but also as individual loving souls of God's creation. We also include angels, both collective in joined alignment within God's energy and love, as well as individual with ever changing purpose. Life too, as a human, is not simplistic; it too is with ever changing reasons and purposes."

I can not say that I have yet grasped the full understanding of that information. I will be taking it in again and again as a breath of love, as a source of information which is endless. The knowledge being given by one, but gained through the experiences of many. Experiences in that collective "we" is us. It is the angels, the guides, the loved ones, Jesus Christ and the saints; the list goes on. With the understanding that there is that oneness beyond as a resource brings my work to a divine level. There is oneness with you; all the readers of this book; all those connected to spirit; we are all able to receive information. We have the soul. When we join that Heavenly alignment, our completed soul's paths and lives become a part of that knowledge that can be read, experienced and tapped into. This brings meaning to all that we do, a need for knowing, acknowledging and accepting what we experience on the path we take. I feel it can be explained in this way as well. If you are a lover of gardening in this lifetime, you are one who can name the plants and intuitively connect to the life within plants. The care of the plants comes as natural knowledge to you. Then you die. I do not know anything at all about plants and then I die and join you in Heaven. Now, I am connected to you and love you as I accept from you all the information and love you have for gardening. I, in turn, could use that life experience you had as you share that energy with me. I can share that information with my loved ones still on earth having their human experience. It is like sending a little green thumb energy from Heaven. We are all connected. Oneness.

CHAPTER 37

Manifesting The Intuitive Power To Receive Direction On Your Path

You are a Psychic Medium living as a prophet in the millennium. You are aware of your soul connection. How important it is to acknowledge your intuition as your most important manifestations.

You do not have to embrace a psychic medium to acknowledge that there is a manifestation of information; this intuitive drawing to yourself the information needed for you. It is with acknowledgment that the psychic medium can accept these improvable manifesting intuitive impressions which are so clear and accurate..They are healing and full of love. There is no doubt that manifestation is a great purpose to all the aspects of life paths and soul missions. You do not need a psychic medium to connect and move along your spiritual path.

How important it is to acknowledge there is a great need to manifest into our lives a sense of security and peace. There is the desire to manifest our dreams into reality. It is a pretty powerful word and tool to use to bring forth what we believe will make us happy or bring contentment to our lives. Manifestation as a noun is defined as a sign or the act of showing something, or as a visible form of spiritual beings. In our world, manifestation needs to be looked at as an action word. It is a constant. We are manifesting and bringing into our lives what is concrete and purposeful at every moment and with every breath. There are signs and demonstrations of manifestation that overlap each other, while combining with other energies as well. To have control over what comes is a perspective which has been described before within specific modalities and techniques, but in truth remains a mystery. What we need to know is the importance of acknowledging something has come to light in our lives on all levels.

Acknowledging manifestation just in definition draws attention to a few topics. You can manifest something into your life; something materialistic and something you want; someone you would like to connect with and so much more. It is believed that you can draw to yourself and manifest any desire or aspiration. For a moment, consider it as an action reflecting directly from what you desire within your heart and mind. This approach is one connected to your inside soul purpose. To clarify, the inside location which needs to awaken to what you are requesting is your soul, your inner spirit, your divine center within your human body. It is the core being which you are manifesting for. This is the space that reminds your heart and your mind that you are here for a purpose and that there are paths for us to follow. Manifesting information this way helps to guide us and may even come to us from a spiritual guide which manifests information to us. We hear about putting "it" out there when you are seeking your inner soul's desire. As a human being it is essential that we put "it" on the inside so it can radiate out into the universal energy with God. Soul acknowledgement is the strongest resource we can draw on to bring that manifestation into our lives. When it is done this way, it feels trustworthy and positive. It will be spiritually enlightening and soul advancing. Why put it out there when satisfaction will be felt within? Bring the energy within and beam it out. It is your soul that is connected to the Highest of the High. Having this connection gives the soul that strength and understanding of what will complete you.

There are things we want and things we don't which seem to manifest. There was a recent great awakening to the idea that we can manifest anything we "want". This concept is both an idea and comes from a combination of resources all providing one desired result. It is the idea that if you "put it out there" it will manifest. It is both a faith-based prospective, as well as a forced creation of energy to produce what you desire. Without putting this concept aside totally, I feel it is a powerful tool of intention, but there is so much more at stake when you take upon yourself an attitude which you can get whatever it is you want. First of all, you may be setting yourself up for disappointment. I have seen time and time again that this concept of putting so much energy to put it "out" there leaves no attraction to yourself. You do have a soul; a soul with a purpose. That purpose may not require, need or desire what it is that you are trying to draw to yourself. There are no coincidences in life, so there is a reasoning why you will or will not get what you want. You will get what you are meant to have. Being open to this concept does draw that expression from inside you. It builds a belief which motivates you and makes you aware of what opportunities might be out there. That is not so much a secret as it is being attentive. It is a common-sense approach to being open to what is out there and not hiding while waiting for it to come to you. While you're waiting for it to come, you may miss out on an action you should have taken or an opportunity you may have overlooked because it required you to be involved in the reaching and receiving. It becomes enlightening once you are more conscious of what you are perceiving. Although letting it out into the "universe" is currently a very popular approach, it is not the only answer to manifestation.

Not often is it spoken about that which is truly meant to be. A desire comes from your soul energy which resides within and acts upon each of our human bodies; what is meant to be, what you are supposed to have, versus what you want. What about the responsibility to give back once you have received? If we are all connected within "oneness" with individuality leading us, shouldn't we consider the needs of others within our own desires? It would be profound if all humans wanted to manifest joy and peace to all. It is common knowledge that when you share energy with others, they can feel it. If you feel joy for someone, they will know, if you love someone, they feel it and send you love in return. By giving of yourself, you manifest in return a natural flow of energy. Love, money and work; all these things flow with a cycle. You can hop in or begin that cycle by sending out from your soul that desire. Being happy for someone else will draw to you the energy of others being happy for you in return. Acknowledging that others are actively living and manifesting for their own lives will bring a connection for you. Each action brings connections to our own paths and to receiving our desires.

Consider your soul purpose, your path in life, the inner knowing that you have. Do you really want something, need something? I ask this on all levels and within all variables including life, love, spirituality, relationships, family, work and more. You are here for a purpose. If you consider another definition of manifestation, it is that sign that something is real and that it can exist within your current lifetime experience. You are a manifestation! You are here for a purpose and that soul desire will be granted if you place it within you. Tell your spirit, your soul, your heart and mind what your plan is and ask for direction. Allow the higher energy in your life to give you, from here or from beyond, what you are supposed to have and realize that there is a reason for where you are right now as well. Don't be surprised; maybe the guidance will come through a spiritual manifestation. Either way, you will be brought that satisfaction for which you yearn. Why take the time to set that thought to manifest free into the energy of the universe to be fulfilled? You are the energy of the universe! You are already connected through your soul to the power that blesses you with life and gave you that very path you seek to follow. Put that request within, spell it out and absorb it. What you need, what your soul longs for, will automatically come to you if it is meant to be. Remembering there is a higher purpose to all that comes, or does not, will bring you an inner peace. Knowing and acknowledging there is a timeline and plan allows for what is perfectly meant for you to experience. You may not even be aware of the complete satisfaction you could receive if you're too busy trying to energetically draw something which you are aware of to come and fill that space first. Faith and trust is needed when attaching to what is manifested.

A second topic to manifestation falls within my line of work. As a psychic medium, and through each session, I am manifesting information. I am receiving something which I am able to take from beyond present and represent it in current time. I am also channeling and manifesting information from souls that have crossed over, as well as any guides or angels that may come through. This manifestation is an actual process of acknowledging there is some information being received for a higher purpose. That purpose being to heal, inform, connect, or enlighten someone along their journey' to give foresight on a present situation and the future it holds within its current status. It could also be the manifestation of a complete guide to a spiritual path to be expressed. It is a beautiful connection to information when it is produced with positive and pure intention. In addition, there is the manifestation from the spiritual realm.

Manifestation, beyond seeking, has a definition that holds great significance when considering the appearance of a soul, angel, guide, or other vision. You can also channel this information through an intuitive impression. This manifesting is the bringing forth of a spiritual being, a Divine connection to information or soul. What is manifested can also be a sign that is interpreted. It is information that has become understood. It can appear as something, or someone called, or who just appeared due to intentional or unintentional invitation. If something has manifested, you have been shown this result and become aware of what has come. I have seen manifestation in photos and videos that have been called ghosts or orbs. These are still the appearance of spirit at that moment making a contact and trying to communicate through 'manifestation.' It is more of a verb than a noun, in my opinion.

This is the action of manifestation. There is still a great sense of understanding and acknowledgment which must be accepted. What is the experience bringing to your life? If you are with a medium or at home, or at a special place and there is contact with the Divine, accept the information. Be your own prophet. Finding purpose within each connection is not necessary. Accepting that you have experiences can bring deeper understanding of why. It is very possible that all that is manifested in your life has a level of profoundness; some very high experiences may shine above others. In this spiritual world it is also important to remember that all is not without purpose. Manifesting does not come without responsibility. If it is you drawing into your life or if it is a manifestation through spirit, there is a common energy, love. There is a connection to all of the energy around us when love is involved.

Take time to connect to and through your soul today!

ABOUT THE AUTHOR

Rebecca Anne LoCicero has been working within the New England area, nationally and worldwide for 20+ years as psychic medium. "Messages from Heaven" her main presentation involving direct, divine and accurate "readings" for the people from their loved ones who have died. Rebecca has an exclusive and unique way to present her messages. She is bold, brassy, honest, loud, outgoing, accurate, hysterically funny and full of joy! She will entertain you and touch your heart as she talks about her connections "here and there" and the passageways in-between.

"If your dead people want to get a message to you they will find me! When we cross over, we retain our free will and our personality and messages will reflect who we truly were! Get ready! You will laugh, cry, scream and shout. It will be soul fulfilling!" (r.a.l)

Rebecca Anne often refers to herself as a "one of a kind" as you never know which outrageous words or references she will bluntly convey to her audience. Clients easily associate to the way she shares the information with honesty to what she is receiving in real world expressions. Currently her presentations are being held in a variety of locations including national comedy clubs such as "The Funny Bone", holistic centers, lecture hall, and expositions as a headliner presenter and more. She can be heard in Massachusetts (WRSI, The River) and throughout Connecticut on mainstream radio monthly as the guest psychic. Blog Talk Radio is the internet radio provider for her personal show. She has appeared on "Better Connecticut" and numerous other local access channel shows.

Her reach goes beyond that as she is a three- time published author and the owner of The Beyond Center, her home base and private office. This is where she teaches classes, holds smaller presentations and groups, produces The Beyond Newsletter, and hosts her own internet Radio Show.

Rebecca Anne is also proud to work as a tested & certified medium through the Forever Family Foundation for the last 8 years. Being in this line of work allows Rebecca Anne to work side by side with many special gifted people. She has lectured alongside motivational speakers and healers *However, Rebecca knows, and is confident, that her reputation stands on her experience and accuracy in this business and knows she can "rock that spirit world" without "associations" to others! "The dead don't care about your social status; they just want to share their unending love with those still here." (r.a.l)